Stoicism:

A Detailed Breakdown on Stoicism Philosophy and Wisdom from the Greats

George Tanner

© 2017

COPYRIGHT

Stoicism: Learn A Detailed Breakdown on Stoicism Philosophy and Wisdom from the Greats

By George Tanner

Copyright @2017 By George Tanner

All Rights Reserved.

The following eBook is reproduced below with the goal of providing information that is as accurate and as reliable as possible. Regardless, purchasing this eBook can be seen as consent to the fact that both the publisher and the author of this book are in no way experts on the topics discussed within, and that any recommendations or suggestions made herein are for entertainment purposes only. Professionals should be consulted as needed before undertaking any of the action endorsed herein.

This declaration is deemed fair and valid by both the American Bar Association and the Committee of Publishers Association and is legally binding throughout the United States.

Furthermore, the transmission, duplication or reproduction of any of the following work, including precise information, will be considered an illegal act, irrespective whether it is done electronically or in print. The legality extends to creating a secondary or tertiary copy of the work or a recorded copy and is only allowed with express written consent of the Publisher. All additional rights are reserved.

The information in the following pages is broadly considered to be a truthful and accurate account of facts, and as such any inattention, use or misuse of the information in question by the reader will render any resulting actions solely under their purview. There are no scenarios in which the publisher or the original author of this work can be in any fashion deemed liable for any hardship or damages that may befall them after undertaking information described herein.

Additionally, the information found on the following pages is intended for informational purposes only and should thus be considered, universal. As befitting its nature, the information presented is without assurance regarding its continued validity or interim quality. Trademarks that mentioned are done without written consent and can in no way be considered an endorsement from the trademark holder.

TABLE OF CONTENTS

INTRODUCTION: 1
HISTORY OF STOICISM 9
THE GOOD LIFE 23
ON CONTROL 31
VIRTUE IN STOICISM 41
STOIC LOGIC AND YOU 50
COSMOLOGY AND THEOLOGY IN STOICISM 62
STOICISM AND PSYCHOLOGY 67
STOICISM AND THE EMOTIONS 79
OUTER TROUBLES; PREVENTATIVE MEASURES IN STOICISM 89
STOIC DISCOMFORT 100
APATHEIA – STOIC INNER PEACE 107
CONCLUSION 113
DESCRIPTION 121

Introduction

For over two thousand years the Stoic school has lived, died and been reborn according to the whims of fortune. In its earliest days, it consisted of a small but precocious group of Greeks pacing the public spaces of Athens, teaching virtue by example and challenging vice with argument and irony. In its middle period, it yawned through the Greek islands and into Anatolia and developed a consistent doctrine which earned it a place among the great schools of ancient philosophy. At its height, it stretched across the Mediterranean, carried by the ships and soldiers of the Roman Empire, and whispered in the ears of statesmen and slaves alike. And when its flame was extinguished with the Empire in which it burned, it lived on through Christian doctrine and belief, a specter floating through the pens and consciousnesses of monks and theologians as they copied and recopied texts and carried its ideas into the modern age.

Today it lives again, first and with the great energy in cognitive behavioral therapy, and second in its own right, as a philosophy whose message resonates in spite of its age. Its emphasis on living well, on attention to others, our community, our planet, meet modern problems at the heart and shift the focus of daily life from living well in the sense of pleasure to living well in the sense of virtue. And as a bonus, Stoicism teaches how to deal with difficult coworkers, to cope with stress, to live according to our values, and to choose values that are becoming of our nature as human beings.

So what is Stoicism? The answer to this question in many ways turns on another question: What is wisdom? Further, what part does wisdom play in our daily lives? For the Stoics, wisdom is the virtue that governs all others. It directs us first to choose our ends, those things for the sake of which we do everything else, and how to pursue those ends. If I am a thief and I come up with a new trick or a subtle way of pilfering what does not belong to me, I am clever because I was inventive in obtaining my goal. But I am not wise because my goal, to take what is not mine, is not just, because it damages both the person from whom I am stealing, insofar as I have hurt them materially, and myself, insofar as I have degraded myself by the practice of a vice. Similarly, if I have a noble end, for example dedicating myself to charity, but in order to carry out this end I take loans and bury myself in unsustainable debt, I am not wise because I acted imprudently in pursuit of my goal. Both justice and prudence are cardinal virtues for the Stoics, and they appear together such that it is impossible to practice one while violating another. Stealing from one person in order to be charitable to another, for example, is neither just nor prudent. It is not just because, as before, it is an injury to myself and to another party, and it is not prudent because it is unjust. Stoicism is that school of philosophy for which wisdom, being for them the state that obtains in a fully developed human nature, is the end of all ethical activity, is the goal of practicing the virtues in correct relationship with one another, and is thus the goal of an ethical life.

Stoicism as an ancient school may be thought in opposition to its rivals. Aristotle's Peripatetic school held that the end goal of an ethical life was *eudaimonia*, which roughly translates as human flourishing. Wisdom and the other virtues were and are important for Aristotelian ethics, but, unlike for the Stoics, they were not sufficient for the good life, nor did they exhaust human happiness—pleasure and a bit of good fortune are also necessary on Aristotle's view. For the Epicureans, another rival school, pleasure is the aim of ethical life, is sufficient for a good life, in particular, the relief of pain. More than any other school, the Epicureans were direct competitors with the Stoics. It might be easy to see why. They are, for example, not as concerned with virtue as either the Peripatetics or the Stoics, and though they also hold wisdom to be a cardinal virtue, prudence, for them correct choices with respect to pleasure and pain, is the center of the virtues.

The love of wisdom is, for the Stoics as with their contemporaries, a life in a state of what may be called a kind of desperation. It is akin to a lover who thinks only of their beloved. In his Symposium, Plato has Socrates say that love lives between humans and their desires. The end of love, the result of the lover's union with their beloved, is reproduction. In the case of people, love's aim is the creation of children. In the case of trades, love's aim is the production of crafts. And in the case of wisdom, the lover seeks to produce and to spread concepts. In a sense, then, the philosopher's goal is always pedagogical. Where possible the philosopher seeks out the truth of the world behind appearances. But not satisfied with keeping knowledge, the philosopher endeavors to spread it through thought and action, to right error by example and fill the gaps of discourse.

Stoicism is a life devoted to this pedagogical discipline. It emphasizes practice, living by example, by teaching the doctrines of Stoicism, particularly ethics, and by exemplifying its doctrines. The Stoics collectively characterize philosophy as *askêsis*, a kind of practice of knowledge concerning the beneficial. Their approach to philosophy was therapeutic;

their emphasis was developing good habits through knowledge of what is and is not to be valued. They aim to strengthen *prohairesis*, the faculty of choice, and to thereby cultivate wisdom, to become Stoic sages.

Maybe the greatest hurdle to the adoption of Stoic ideas is how few of their works are extant. This is a problem not at all uncommon when interpreting classical thinkers. We have lists of works written by Epicurus, Aristotle and Zeno, provided to us by authors like Diogenes Laertius, very few of which survive, if any. We can nonetheless build accurate, if not always consistent, accounts of what these thinkers say. For the Stoics in particular, our main references are Roman philosophers like Epictetus, Seneca, Plutarch, and Cicero, and, of course, Marcus Aurelius. They preserved the core of Stoicism, and in a way that engages with their peers and draws on a wealth of social and historical examples. It is to these Roman thinkers that I will turn in exploring Stoicism here, and from the examples given at the height of the Roman Empire.

Stoicism's heart and goal is a life in accordance with nature. As Emperor Marcus Aurelius says in book six of his *Meditations*,

"In conformity to the nature of the universe, every single thing is accomplished, for certainly it is not in conformity to any other nature that each thing is accomplished, either a nature which externally comprehends this or a nature which is comprehended within this nature, or a nature external and independent of this."[1]

The Stoic idea of nature is different than the modern idea. Both instinct and inheritance play a role, like our modern concept, but they include the full development of a thing in their conversation. What is the Stoic idea of nature? If I, for example, asked "what is the nature of this seed?" you may answer "to become a tree." Your answer accords with the idea of nature the Stoics employ; the seed's nature is not just an embryo contained in a coat with its nutrients, but also that it will become a tree when conditions pertain. Similarly, an individual may steal, lie, cheat and practice infidelity because of some evolutionary adaptation, and an undeveloped person may have these behaviors as part of their nature, but also part of their nature is the capacity to grow beyond these limits, to become rationally and morally developed. The former is a life of animality for the Stoics. As Epictetus says in book one, chapter six of his *Discourses*,

---

[1] Marcus Aurelius, *Meditations*, book six

"What, then, are these things done in us only. Many, indeed, in us only, of which the rational animal had peculiar need; but you will find many common to us with irrational animals. Do they them understand what is done? By no means. For use is one thing, and understanding is another: God had need of irrational animals to make use of appearances, but of us to understand the use of appearances. It is, therefore, enough for them to eat and to drink, and to sleep and to copulate, and to do all the other things which they severally do. But for us, to whom He has given also the faculty, these things are not sufficient; for unless we act in a proper and orderly manner, and conformably to the nature and constitution of each thing, we shall never attain our true end."[2]

If a seed that never becomes a tree can be said to have failed in its nature, so too can a person who never develops morally be said to have failed.

Moral maturity implies a life cultivated by and in virtue. For this reason, the virtues in Stoic doctrine guide action. The cardinal Stoic virtues are courage, temperance, prudence, and justice. Without these, life is animalistic, unworthy of the name "human." There is no easy path or royal road to this life.

---

[2] Epictetus, *Discourses,* book one, chapter six

Stoicism demands a foundation of good habits and a critical disposition. And such a character is precisely what Stoicism aims to cultivate.

HISTORY OF STOICISM

Among the ranks of the Stoics are scientists, craftsmen, merchants, farmers, politicians—people from every corner of society. What brings them together is their commitment to virtue, their common ethical and intellectual origin, and the practice of Stoic living. Stoicism, like other Western traditions, has its origins in Greece. Their founder is Zeno of Citium. Neither his nor the works of his most famous successor of the same period, Chrysippus, survive. Scholars across the ages have nonetheless constructed an account of their lives from testimony and existing evidence. I can, using their conclusions, give a general history of the origins of Stoic philosophy and its development.

Zeno was born in Cyprus the same year Alexander the Great was, around 336 B.C.E. He was the son of a merchant, and himself became a merchant when he was of age. In one account, in his 20s he experienced a tragic shipwreck, which marked the end of his life at sea. On another account, he was already in Athens when he learned that one of his shipments was lost to the waves. On either account, in Athens he was introduced to Xenophon's Memorabilia, and from it the character of Socrates, whom he admired. Later, he studied under Crates of Thebes and Stilpon of Megara, philosophers of the Cynic school (the same school to which Diogenes of Synope belonged). Accounts from Diogenes Laertius say that he greeted the shipwreck as an act of good fortune because it allowed him to shed his old life and devote himself to the study of philosophy.

Zeno is famous for teaching in the Stoa Poikile or Painted Porch, a central location in Athens where the bounty from distant wars was displayed for the public. It is after this porch that the Stoics would be named, but their original name was the "Zenonians." In the Stoa Poikile, Zeno discussed virtue and its superiority over pleasure and described a natural law which held precedence over the random swerve of atoms. Both the position that pleasure was the good and that randomly moving atoms were the governing principle of the universe was held by the Epicureans. Zeno also lived his teachings, and he was praised throughout his life for his consistency and his prudence.

Zeno lived and taught in Athens for the remainder of his life. His death is said to be akin to that of Diogenes of Sinope. As an old man, after breaking a toe, he declared himself satisfied with the life he had lived and strangled himself to death. The story may be apocryphal, but it exemplifies his strength of will, his good character, and his self-discipline.

Zeno was followed by Cleanthes, son of Phanias, a native of Assos. Diogenes Laertius tells us Cleanthes began life as a pugilist who arrived in Athens with only four drachmas to his name. Upon meeting Zeno, he adopted a life of philosophical study. He was known for being industrious, driven by his extreme poverty to work his entire life. At night he drew water in gardens belonging to the wealthy and by day he exercised his mind via rigorous argumentation. In his time he was known as a second Heracles, a notable Presocratic philosopher, because of his lean and modest lifestyle and his serious temperament. When he could not afford the paper on which to record Zeno's lectures, he is said to instead have used oyster-shells and the bones of oxen. When Zeno died, Cleanthes carried forward the Zenoian tradition in his teaching and writings.

Cleanthes too died when he was ready. He is said to have suffered from inflammation of his gums, perhaps an account of gingivitis, and was advised by his doctors to forego eating for two days. When the treatment proved successful, his doctors told him that he could resume his diet, but Cleanthes refused. According to him, his life had been long enough, and he was content to end it on his terms. He fasted for the remainder of his days until his death and is said to have died at the same age Zeno had before him.

A whole generation after Zeno washed up on the Athenian shore, in 280 B.C.E., Chrysippus of Soli, the third head of the Zenoian school, was born. Diogenes Laertius says Chrysippus' father, Apollonius, left him a fortune, which he later lost defending himself against legal trouble. It was his misfortune which led him to philosophy, as was the case with Zeno. Chrysippus studied at Plato's Academy and studies physics, rhetoric, and dialectic. He then studied under Cleanthes. When Cleanthes died, Chrysippus inherited Zeno's legacy and became the head of the Stoic school.

In his lifetime Chrysippus wrote over 700 scrolls, none of which survive. In them, he wrote about ethics, physics, logic and argumentation, epistemology and cosmology. He drew extensively from the testimony of other thinkers, so much so that he was often mocked, alleged by his rivals to have nothing of his own to contribute, or that, if his citations were removed from his works, their pages would be blank. His writing style was mirrored in his arguments. It was not seldom that he argued in favor of both positions in a debate and even professed absurd positions if he thought they had pedagogical merit. His students and his opponents alike were baffled and frustrated by his behavior. But we might not find it strange if we remember that Socrates, too, used irony and claimed positions which he did not believe if he thought something could thereby be learned.

Much of what is today called Stoic logic, which we will discuss at length in a later chapter, was developed by Chrysippus. Chrysippus' logic is an ancient alternative to Aristotelian logic and is similar to modern propositional logic pioneered by Gottlob Frege. Chrysippus' logic is at the heart of Stoic advances in science and mathematics, and formalized the notion of "disjunction." Diogenes Laertius noted 118 logical texts penned under Chrysippus' name, seven alone of which tackled the Liar's Paradox. Chrysippus believed that a rigorous ethical system required a foundation in logic and reason, these being the guideposts for everything that exists.

The middle Stoics did not significantly advance the school, so we will only talk briefly about them here. Panaetius, son of Nicagoras, was born almost a century after Chrysippus, in about 180 B.C.E. He studied under Crates of Mallus, a prominent linguist, and then under Critolaus and Carneades before studying under the Stoic philosopher Diogenes of Babylon. His principle work was in ethics, where he argued that physics, not logic, was the starting point of philosophy, and that ethics should be formulated such that even the layman could meet its ends. After him lived Posidonius "the

Athlete," born in Apamea in northern Syria around 135 B.C.E. He continued Posidonius' school in Rhodes where he taught both Greek and Roman scholars. He worked on philosophy, science, and history in his lifetime, but he held the Aristotelian view that philosophy was the master of the other two, directing their aims and ambitions and grounding their conclusions. He is responsible for the metaphor of the topoi or Stoic disciplines, calling physics the meat and blood, logic the bones and tendons, and ethics the soul.

The late Stoics get their start about 100 years after the middle Stoic period. Stoicism found a new home in the Roman Empire, its most famous proponents being Epictetus, Seneca, Cicero, and Marcus Aurelius. Athens sent a delegation of the three major schools—the Academics, the Stoics and the Peripatetics—to Rome around 155 B.C.E. The initial envoy was unsuccessful, earning a backlash from the ruling class in Rome. 70 years later, in around 86 B.C.E., Greek philosophy finally found a home in the Empire with the establishment of Stoic and Epicurean schools.

Epictetus was born around 55 C.E. at Hierapolis, Phrygia. His name means "gained" or "acquired," signifying his birth as a slave. He was allowed by his master to study philosophy with Musonius Rufus, and influential Stoic sage, which bolstered his mind and his reputation. Around 68 C.E. he gained his freedom and began his life teaching philosophy in Rome. When in around 93 C.E. Emperor Domitian banished the philosophers, Epictetus moved to Nicopolis in Greece and there founded his school.

Epictetus believed that self-knowledge is at the center of philosophy, and, following Socrates, that the first aim of philosophical discourse is self-examination. To quote him directly on the matter, from book one, chapter fifteen of his *Discourses*,

"When a man was consulting him how he should persuade his brother to cease being angry with him, Epictetus replied: Philosophy does not propose to secure for a man any external thing. If it did philosophy would be allowing something which is not within its province. For as the carpenter's material is wood, and that of the statuary is copper, so the matter of the art of living is each man's life. "What then is my brother's?" That again belongs to his own art; but with respect to yours, it is one of the external things, like a piece of land, like health, like reputation. But Philosophy promises none of these. "In every circumstance, I will maintain," she says, "the governing part conformable to nature." Whose governing part? "His in whom I am," she says."³

Good alone, he says, is desirable, in opposition to rival schools that in one way or another emphasized pleasure's place in a fulfilled life. It is philosophy's job to provide the standard for good and evil, a task in its ability because both the mind and its products are, he says, of everything in creation, the only things entirely within our influence. When aware of the difference between these poles, an awareness that is based both on knowledge and habit, the wise person will be subject to the rightful order of the world.

What we have of Epictetus' works are not his own writings but lectures and discussions recorded by his student Arrian. Arrian says that Epictetus was the kind of speaker who could cause people to feel what he wanted them to feel when he wanted them to feel it. Arrian says that Epictetus lived a simple life, owning very few things, and though he never married, he adopted the child of a friend in his old age. He died around 135 C.E. of natural causes, having been admired in life by all who knew him.

---

3   Epictetus, *Discourses,* book one, chapter nine

Seneca was born around the turn of the 1st century C.E. in Cordoba, modern-day Spain. He became a citizen of Rome around 5 C.E., carried there by his mother's stepsister. Much of his early life is obscure to us, the evidence for it being scant. What we do know about him is primarily from after his rise to prominence within the Empire. Between C.E. 54 to C.E. 62, he acted as adviser to Nero. On the strength of his abilities in that position, he was also appointed consul in 56 C.E., an important political position in the Empire. Seneca is said to have played an important role in Boudica's rebellion in the recently conquered British territories by forcing loans onto the indigenous aristocracy before calling them in swiftly and with force. This episode may have contributed to the end of his political career.

Seneca wrote both philosophy and plays in his lifetime, in addition to his political writing. Much of his philosophical writing focuses on death and suffering and what one should do to defend oneself against grief and despair. His philosophy was decidedly Stoic, though he did have some eclectic influences, including Plato and the Aristotelians. Seneca wrote tragedies principally, including famous works like Agamemnon, Thyestes and Oedipus. The theme of many of his plays was revenge, a theme adopted by later playwrights influenced by Seneca like Shakespeare, Corneille, and Racine.

In 65 C.E. Seneca was ordered to kill himself by Emperor Nero on suspicion that he plotted to have the Emperor killed. Following tradition, he severed several of his veins in order to bleed to death. It is both unclear and unlikely that he had any involvement in the plot. Nonetheless, his death was slow and painful, owing to his advanced age and purportedly poor diet. In his will, he ordered that his body be cremated without funeral rites.

Cicero was born in 106 B.C.E. in Arpinium, south of Rome. His father was of the equestrian order, a propertied class below senators in Roman society, and thereby possessed a number of privileges and connections beyond the common citizen. From an early age, he learned both Latin and Greek by studying philosophers, rhetoricians, historians, and poets. Cicero used his bilingual tongue to translate and preserve many Greek texts, a proclivity in part responsible for his overwhelming influence during the Renaissance and the enlightenment.

Cicero is purported to have been a bright student who garnered attention from all corners of Roman society. It was little surprise, then, when he pursued a career in politics. He served both Gnaeus Pompeius Strabo and Lucius Cornelius Sulla in their campaigns in the Social War. Later, around 83

B.C.E., he began a career in law. His first major victory is recorded in 80 B.C.E. when he defended Sextus Roscius from the charge of patricide, a particularly serious case and a thorny matter in Roman society. In its aftermath, potentially to avoid the wrath of the dictator Sulla, whose allies Cicero had proven responsible for the murder of Roscius' father, Cicero traveled to Greece and Anatolia. In Athens, he studied with Antiochus of Ascalon, the founder of Middle Platonism, and in Anatolia he studied with leading rhetoricians, perfecting his skills as an orator.

In the conflict between Julius Caesar and Pompey, Cicero favored Pompey as the defender of Rome's Republican tradition. He was then forced to flee Rome when Caesar invaded Italy. He traveled with Pompey's forces for a time, at the same time losing faith in the Pompeian side. When Caesar won the civil war, Cicero returned to Rome and was pardoned. He did not participate in Caesar's assassination but was sympathetic to the cause. Mark Antony during the Second Triumvirate, however, in seeking revenge for Caesar's death, ordered Cicero killed because of his popularity and reputation. Cicero is reported to have, upon his capture, said: "There is nothing proper about what you are doing, soldier, but do try to kill me properly."

Marcus Aurelius was born the great-grandson of a praetor, the grandson of a patrician, reared in an extraordinarily wealthy family that had produced Emperors in the past. His father having died early, Marcus was raised by his grandfather, who taught him good character and the avoidance of bad temper. Marcus was taught at home by a number of tutors, including a leading Homeric scholar. After a hemorrhage, then Emperor Hadrian adopted Marcus' father-in-law with the intention that Marcus should rise to the throne. Even upon his appointment to serve under Antoninus, the consul for the year 139 C.E. and successor to Hadrian following the death of Marcus' father-in-law, Marcus is said to have acted with the same thrift and solemnity in his public role as when he was a private citizen.

As an Emperor, Marcus exercised and exemplified the Stoic virtues, earning the reputation as the last of the Five Good Emperors from Machiavelli. Marcus was proficient in imperial administration, versed in legislative theory. He commanded the Roman legions in several wars in his lifetime, with the Germanic tribes, with Parthia, and against the Marcomanni and the Sarmatians. During his campaigns he wrote his Meditations, a masterwork of philosophy still read widely by politicians and generals because of its wisdom in both political and military affairs, as well as its applicability to daily life.

Marcus Aurelius died in Vindobona, modern-day Vienna, on March 17th 180. Despite his orders, his ashes were returned to Rome, to Hadrian's mausoleum. There a column was built to commemorate his victories against the Germans and Sarmatians. His son Commodus succeeded him to the throne, despite the latter's unpredictable behavior and poor training in both politics and the military. It was nonetheless necessary that Commodus come to the throne to preserve peace in the Empire, to prevent another of the many succession wars in Roman history from tearing the Empire asunder.

The Roman Stoics emphasized therapeutic and theoretical aims over ethical and political activity, but almost all of the notable Roman figures were involved in politics in some capacity. Cato the Younger served as military tribune, praetor, and was a powerful opponent of Julius Caesar. Cicero, serving as a Roman Consul, taught himself Stoic ideas as one of the many schools he studied in his eclectic approach to philosophy. Athenodorus and Arius were counselors to Augustus Caesar. Seneca advised Nero. And Marcus Aurelius, of course, was Caesar of Rome. Covering each of these thinkers in detail is a task beyond the scope of this book;

they each deserve their own book, chronicling their thoughts and deeds. I will nonetheless draw from several of them in this work.

This brief account of their history has shown that the Stoic school is diverse and malleable and has lived in many vastly different circumstances through its iterations. How are they all united? What allows them to keep the same name, despite the diversity in doctrine within the school? All Stoics accept the three topoi, ethics, logic, and physics. Their all teach virtue with the aim of living in accordance with human nature. Their logical systems include both the modern, formal definition, the study of what consequences follow from what premises, and epistemic concerns, concerns about the nature of knowledge and what human beings can know. Stoic physics includes the modern sense of the word, encompassing a variety of natural sciences, and metaphysics and theology. For the Stoics, the gods and the soul were physical beings, and studying them revealed their governing principles. This book will teach the nuts and bolts of all aspects of the *topoi* and will serve as a general introduction to Stoic ideas and practice.

THE GOOD LIFE

"What is good?" This question is at the center of ethics. Before an ethical system can be constructed, criteria need to be established. For the ancients, and for many modern ethicists as well, the distinction between good and bad depend on life's aim. Those choices which approach or are in accord with life's aim are good. Those choices which frustrate or miss life's aim are bad. I mentioned in the introduction that the aim of the Stoic life is agreement with nature. That lifestyle and those actions that agree with fully developed human nature are virtuous, and those that do not are vicious. In this chapter, we will explore what "living in agreement or accord with nature" means in detail, virtue, and vice in general, and good and evil in particular. The goal is to ground your perceptions and your character in an unshakable foundation. As Epictetus says in book three, chapter six of his Discourses:

"The good man is invincible, for he does not enter the contest where he is not stronger. If you want to have his land and all that is on it, take the land; take his slaves, take his magisterial office, take his poor body. But you will not make his desire fail in that which it seeks, nor his aversion fall into that which he would avoid. The only contest into which he enters is that about things which are within the power of his will; how then will he not be invincible?"[4]

The Stoics think that, fundamentally, what is good exists in two places. First, a person may be good if they are well developed—if they are virtuous in character. Second, a person's choices may be good if, by choosing, he or she is exercising virtue. In the case of inner virtue, a person must develop a stable or durable disposition, such that their character endures life's tempests. In choice, a person must make a habit of virtuous activity, and this activity must be motivated by their virtuous character. If for example, one acts courageously because they do not know the danger of their situation, they are not for that reason good. If one is aware of the danger, that they may even be killed for pursuing a certain course but are directed by wisdom to uphold their duty, then their action is good.

There is a derivative sense of virtue in Stoicism which concerns objects. Whether or not choosing some sought after thing is virtuous is determined by generalization. Is it true that choosing the desired object is in all cases beneficial? In other words, does it always help people develop as human

---

4   Epictetus, *Discourses,* book three, chapter six

beings? This is not the case for money and power, for example. In the case of money, stories abound of spoiled children, corrupt businesses, and celebrity debauchery. Power gives those who would otherwise not act in untoward ways, though their character may be poor, license to practice their evil inclinations. We can extend these examples to a number of other possessions and trappings. Celebrity for its own sake gives the undisciplined spirit license to practice vanity. And security without fortitude, inner security against vice, invites sloth and indolence. Pleasure also does not meet this criterion. Against the Epicureans, for whom pleasure was life's aim, the Stoics argue that there are many pleasures that do not cultivate the individual. Knowledge, for example, considered a mental pleasure by Epicurus, may excite anger in an individual and thereby undermine their decision making. And in cases where pleasures do not make a person worse, they still may not make that person better. A choice of objects of this kind may be indifferent, but it is not virtuous. We should remember Epictetus' words when considering the difference between what is good and what is indifferent, and take to heart the reason for this distinction. In Chapter eight, book three of his *Discourses* he says,

"As we exercise ourselves against sophistical questions, so we ought to exercise ourselves daily against appearances; for these appearances also propose questions to us. "A certain person son is dead." Answer: the thing is not within the power of the will: it is not an evil. "A father has disinherited a certain son. What do you think of it?" It is a thing beyond the power of the will, not an evil. "Caesar has condemned a person." It is a thing beyond the power of the will, not an evil. "The man is afflicted at this." Affliction is a thing which depends on the will: it is an evil. He has borne the condemnation bravely." That is a thing within the power of the will: it is a good. If we train ourselves in this manner, we shall make progress; for we shall never assent to anything of which there is not an appearance capable of being comprehended."[5]

This discussion allows us to clarify a distinction not always made, between good and evil, virtue and vice, and positive and negative. For the Stoics, only choices can be good or evil. For example, in the previous paragraph, we looked at money, power, and pleasure and considered the value of pursuing them. But it is not money, power, or pleasure themselves that are good or indifferent, but our relationship to them. As Marcus Aurelius says in book six of his Meditations,

---

[5]   Epictetus, *Discourses*, book three, chapter eight

"The substance of the universe is obedient and compliant; and the reason which governs it has in itself no cause for doing evil, for it has no malice, nor does it do evil to anything, nor is anything harmed by it. But all things are made and perfected according to this reason."[6]

If we choose money over virtue, our choice is a bad one. Similarly, Stoics call another person's actions good or evil based on the choice involved.

When not a particular decision by a particular human being, choices are either virtuous or vicious. Those choices which are consistent with nature, that are good for any person, are virtuous. Choices such as these are directed by a well-developed faculty of choice and thereby called prudent or wise. Those choices that are inconsistent with human nature, that in some way degrade our character, are vicious. Choices such as these are made hastily and out of ignorance, thus they earn the name folly. Returning to the money example, if I cheat someone out of their life savings, I act evilly. But if I consider the choice of cheating someone out of their money abstractly, I judge that kind of action to be vicious. We will

---

[6] Marcus Aurelius, *Meditations,* book five

discuss virtue and vice further in the chapter dedicated to them.

Money, power, and pleasure outside the context of either concrete or abstract choices are externals. Externals can be positive, neutral, or negative. Positive externals are in some way fitting to our nature as human beings. Money, power, and pleasure may be positive externals in the right circumstances, for example, if the acquisition of money allows you to exercise prudence. They may also be neutral. Even of other people, Marcus Aurelius says in book five of the *Meditations*,

"In one respect man is the nearest thing to me, so far as I must do good to men and endure them. But so far as some men make themselves obstacles to my proper acts, man becomes to me one of the things which are indifferent, no less than the sun or wind or a wild beast. Now it is true that these may impede my action, but they are no impediments to my effects and disposition, which have the power of acting conditionally and changing."[7]

Negative externals are inconsistent with the nature of rational beings. The particular bad choices of others, while evil from

---

7   ibid

the perspective of choice, are also negative from the perspective of externals. Money, power, and pleasure may also be negative under the right circumstances. If your money would allow you to act in a vicious way, it is a negative external. We will discuss externals at length in the chapter on what is and is not in our power.

To round off our discussion of good and bad, let us now look at the place of true and false judgments in determining value. The Stoics think that correct judgments about choices and externals affect how we feel. A well-developed character and faculty of choice knows the difference between virtue and vice in choice and positive and negative in externals. Further, the development of one's judgment is itself an object of morality. If I am not well developed, if I consistently choose externals over virtue, or choose externals that harm my character, I have bad judgment. Correct and incorrect judgments are products of my understanding of physics and logic. This is why the Stoics think physics and logic, the other two *to poi*, are necessary for a life in accordance with nature.

Correct judgments about choices also require that one knows what is in their power and what is not. Desiring what is not in one's power is not only contrary to nature, it is also a strain on human flourishing and an obstacle to a happy life. It is necessary, therefore, for you to learn what is and is not in your power if you are to transform Stoic moral theory into practical morality.

ON CONTROL

Fresh out of college, I had a lot on my plate. There were too many bills to count, too many job applications to apply for, and too many family members to satisfy. In six months I would have to begin loan repayments, and the local servicer was not shy in reminding me of the interest accumulating. Despite coming through the meat-grinder of higher education unscathed, I was more stressed than I'd ever been in college, with the exception of a few, dreadful finals weeks.

My solution was to bury my head in the sand. Though I applied for positions, and eventually landed one, I also avoided opening those friendly reminder letters, skirted several bill payments, and ran from the topic of my future goals. I managed in that period, but I did not live well. The best part of my day was the hours spent on the couch watching television after work, and only because I could avoid thinking about the cold steel in my chest every time an unknown number appeared on my caller id. In truth, I was miserable.

The deeper the ditch, the more rainwater it holds. My gradual, but consistent, retreat from responsibility left me bathed in rainwater without an umbrella. It was quick, but when the storm came, it was relentless. I'm embarrassed to say that I went without a phone for a while, I was trapped making large repayments, and I had been isolated from my family when I needed them most. And perhaps the worst part of it was that it was avoidable. I could have renegotiated my loans, I could have kept in touch with my family, and I could have budgeted my savings, but I didn't. I had goofed.

In his Enchiridion, the Roman Stoic Epictetus compares life to a play. No matter the circumstances we find ourselves in, he says, we must give the best performance we can. It would have been nice if I were born rich. Because most of my problems were money related, it would have saved me from drowning in my mess. But I also could have saved myself. Though the part handed to me wasn't ideal, I had messed up the performance. Specifically, I had not, under the weight of my burdens, shown resilience; I broke.

I failed in this instance because I did not recognize what was and what was not in my power. Marcus Aurelius says in book five of his *Meditations*,

"Things themselves touch not the soul, not in the least degree; nor have they admission to the soul, nor can they turn or move the soul: but the soul turns and moves itself alone, and whatever judgments it may think proper to make, such it makes for itself the things which present themselves to it."[8]

What is and is not in our power is a central Stoic theme and the heart of their ethics. To put it another way, the Stoics call us to recognize what we control and what we do not. It was in my power to do all of the above, though they may not have turned out well anyway. It was also in my power to regulate my reaction to misfortune. Even of those problems that were unavoidable, I had the power to steel myself by recognizing that their outcomes didn't belong to me, by recognizing that they were externals.

Why is this distinction important? Epictetus says that if we are invested in what we do not control, then we invite unhappiness. This, he thinks, is akin to slavery because our well being is at the mercy of either other people or fate. If we leave ourselves open to external influences, it is as though we are inviting strangers into our home and expecting them to care for it when we do not even care for it ourselves.

There are three classes of things which Epictetus thinks are in our control. Opinions and judgments are the first. We are capable of changing our opinions when they are ill-formed

---

[8] Marcus Aurelius, *Meditations*, book five

and reassessing our judgments when they are incorrect. Choices and actions are the second. Both the development of our faculty of choice, our prohairesis, and our concrete decisions are at the core of who we are as individuals. Desires and aversions are the third. What we do, what we choose, influences our desires, as do our experiences. But if a desire is harmful, we can choose to avoid it, to wean ourselves off it, or to seek help in doing so.

Nothing else is in our control. Epictetus discusses poverty, disease, and death, for example. In part, these things are in our control. If I exercise and eat well, I can perhaps stave off disease and delay death. And if I do no work at all, poverty is almost guaranteed. But I cannot avoid death altogether—doing so is beyond my power. Similarly, I can take the greatest care in my hygiene and my health and still become sick, even fatally ill, from genetic diseases, cancer, or an inopportune handshake.

One pitfall Epictetus identifies lies in identifying oneself with one's possessions. We might recognize this today in various brand wars. Pepsi versus Coke, Apple versus Microsoft, GM or Ford versus a foreign car manufacturer—there are many tribes along brand lines. But we do not control the integrity of these brands or the quality of their products, unless, perhaps, you are an executive at one of these companies. Similarly, one might be complimented on their home, their clothes, or their cellphone. Even the love of knowledge and books can leave us vulnerable. Epictetus draws attention to this in book four chapter four of his *Discourses* when he says,

"Remember that not only the desire of power and of riches makes us mean and subject to others, but even the desire of tranquility, and of leisure. and of traveling abroad, and of learning. For, to speak plainly, whatever the external thing may be, the value which we set upon it places us in subjection to others. What, then, is the difference between desiring, to be a senator or not desiring to be one; what is the difference between desiring power or being content with a private station; what is the difference between saying, "I am unhappy, I have nothing, to do, but I am bound to my books as a corpse"; or saying, "I am unhappy, I have no leisure for reading"? For as salutations and power are things external and independent of the will, so is a book."[9]

But being complimented, or maligned, for these objects does not amount to a personal compliment or slight. You're not being called a good person because you have a nice cell

---

9   Epictetus, *Discourses,* book four, chapter four

phone. Epictetus gives a horse as an example. If a horse thinks of itself as handsome, it would make sense for a beautiful horse. But if you think that, because you have a beautiful horse, you're hot stuff, you're prideful of something that is not yours. That horse can be taken away; it belongs to you in title alone.

Epictetus thinks that we should limit what we consume. You may take pleasure in good food, fast cars, and nice clothes. I do, too. But if we indulge in these things, we open ourselves to desiring them. We give up some of our control to luxuries whose possession is not entirely our own. If we make ourselves vulnerable in this way, then we also make ourselves vulnerable to hurt if we lack them. In book three, chapter one of his Discourses Epictetus says:

"'Thus, then, have we many masters?' We have: for we have circumstances as masters prior to our present masters; and these circumstances are many. Therefore it must of necessity be that those who have the power over any of these circumstances must be our masters. For no man fears Caesar himself, but he fears death, banishment, deprivation of his property, prison, and disgrace. Nor does any man love Caesar, unless Caesar is a person of great merit, but he loves wealth, the office of tribune, praetor or consul. When we love, and hate, and fear these things, it must be that those who have the power over them must be our masters. Therefore we adore them even as gods; for we think that what possesses the power of conferring the greatest advantage on us is divine."[10]

Unfortunately, most people leave themselves open to these desires and their accompanying pains. Whereas they should invest emotionally in only those things in their control, most people show slavish devotion to innumerable in differents. In doing so, they let those things in which they should take pride, their choices, desires, and opinions, atrophy.

Employing warfare as a metaphor, Epictetus says that we should not enter any battle we have not already won. By embracing those things that are in our control, we win the battle for happiness before it's waged. Those things in our control do not admit opposition not of our own doing. Those things not in our control can require we vie with innumerable external factors, against none of which we are guaranteed of victory. And even if we to some degree obtain our desires, we may be yet unhappy. Epictetus thinks that even few external goods are enough for the person who wants nothing not in his control. But those who desire a lot, who want wealth, fame,

---

10   Epictetus, *Discourses*, book three, chapter one

and fortune, are too often never satisfied. Though they win battles, their campaigns do not succeed.

In his Discourses, Epictetus describes what we gain from proper attention to those things in and those things beyond our power. He describes the state that emerges from being attached only to what is in your power as tranquility. Progress toward tranquility is measured by the extent to which you're withdrawn from externals. You turn to your own will, to your own faculties, to that part of you which is most you. And in doing so, you exercise this innermost part. By labor, you improve it so that it conforms to human nature. This is the path to freedom. With it comes faithfulness and modesty. Epictetus says that if someone gave you away as a slave, you would be rightfully angry. Giving yourself away is what you do with your mind when you tie your well being to external things.

But what about those things that are assigned to us, though not belonging to us in the sense of being affected by our disposition or our will? For example, to what extent should I care for my son? If he does not take a bath, is failing in school, or is acting in untoward ways, to what extent am I responsible for his actions, and how do I differentiate that responsibility from those things that are or are not in my power? The Stoics here recognize duties. There are situations whose outcomes are not in my control, but there is an extent to which I am responsible, to which I can act, such that abrogation of that responsibility is an injury to myself. In the case of my son, though I cannot defeat fortune in the outcomes of my parenting, I can influence it by my action or inaction.

Similarly, I may have duties to my community. Like the temperament of our children, our parents, and sometimes even our friends and spouses, I cannot control the environment into which I am born. But I do not have to be impassive. Epictetus says in his Enchiridion,

"Duties are universally measured by relations. Is anyone a father? If so, it is implied that the children should take care of him, submit to him in everything, patiently listen to his reproaches, his correction. But he is a bad father. Are you naturally entitled, then, to a good father? No, only to a father. Is a brother unjust? Well, keep your own situation towards him. Consider not what he does, but what you are to do to keep your own faculty of choice in a state conformable to nature."

We saw in the brief historical sketch that it was not uncommon for the Stoics, particularly the later Stoics, to be involved in politics. How do we square this with the doctrine of control? It helps to think about our political responsibilities in relation to our concentric circles of care or concern. The innermost circle, consisting of our immediate family, is considered by the Stoics the most important. As the circle expands, to friends, to neighbors, to countrymen, and to the whole of humanity, our concern becomes more distant, our attachment more remote. Developing our concern to the limits of the circle is, for the Stoics, a kind of development of our sense of justice. It is not difficult to treat our family and our friends in a way becoming of their circumstances, that fulfills what they are owed. It is far more difficult, and a test that we live by principle, to treat strangers with equanimity. On this point, remember the words of Emperor Marcus Aurelius from book three of his Meditations:

"For the lot which is assigned to each man is carried along with him and carries him along with it. And he remembers also that every rational animal is his kinsman, and that to care for all men is according to man's nature, and a man should hold on to the opinion not of all, but of those only who confessedly live according to nature."[11]

---

[11]   Marcus Aurelius, *Meditations*, book three

Virtue in Stoicism

The Stoics think that virtue, moral goodness, is not just sufficient for happiness, it's necessary. In his Stoic Paradoxes, Cicero says that if you value something other than virtue, you will eventually be unhappy. What happiness you may derive from externals is not genuine, both because it is founded upon the mere appearance of what is good for you, and because it is flimsy, fleeting. Happiness built upon externals is subject to fortune, while that happiness which comes from virtue is self-sufficient.

Understanding virtue is both a cognitive and a practical state of being. One must know the character of the virtues, their description, and the distinction between them in order to practice them. But likewise one must know them in practice, through habit and application, to fully grasp their meaning. Cicero says that if we have an interwoven conceptual and experiential map of the virtues, we will also understand why happiness is impossible without them.

Zeno says that each virtue is a kind of wisdom. What exactly he meant by this sparked a debate between his successors, Cleanthes and Chrysippus. Cleanthes thought that all the virtues were wisdom. To put it another way, he thought that in every circumstance where we exercise, prudence, courage, temperance, etc, what we are really exercising is wisdom in different circumstances. Chrysippus thought that each virtue was a type or branch of wisdom. For him, the virtues really were distinct, and they receive the name "virtues" because wisdom is their common property.

Their meaning might become apparent if we consider them carefully. First Cleanthes. If all the virtues are one in the way he means, what is, for example, courage? Courage would be in part a kind of knowledge about what is and is not to be feared and how we should behave in the face of that which threatens us. The other half of courage would be knowledge about the exercise of this first knowledge; a kind of second-order knowledge. But what can we say about the difference between this knowledge and, say, prudence or practical wisdom? They would both be a kind of knowledge, and the object of both kinds, in the second-order version, is a correct exercise of that knowledge. But is everything which we call prudence also courage? What of returning to my friend something he has loaned? Should we say that there is no difference between the correct choice in circumstances like this and those in which my life or my well-being is in danger? I might need new friends if the prospect of returning what is owed to them is a source of disturbance!

What, then, if we do consider the virtues as separate as Chrysippus would, but as all branches or kinds of wisdom instead of all being the same wisdom but in different circumstances? This view seems to more accurately describe the relationship between the virtues as an interconnected we. Under this view, we can explain why, for example, prudence without justice is not a virtue: In the case, I might choose correctly how to carry out some or another aim, but that aim is something like murder or theft. I am therefore wise with respect to my execution, but unwise in what I desire to do. It is for the sake of examples like these, and in fidelity to the kinds of behavior we refer to in English when we use the words "wise" "prudent" and "just," that I will assume Chrysippus' explanation of the relationship between the virtues from here forward.

The Stoics hold that human nature has certain propensities (oikeiôsis) for moral development. Beyond being fully developed human nature, virtue is a state toward which we unconsciously, maybe even by instinct, tend. When we learn to reason during and after childhood, we can then refine our instincts through habituation.

The Stoics identify three drives belonging to every human. First, we act to achieve our goals and interests. These include wealth, security, health, etc. Second, we identify with the interests of others. We start with our immediate family, then our friends, fellow citizens, and finally humanity as a whole. Third, we reason about and solve the problems facing us in life. These drives or propensities require the virtues if they're to be successful. We need courage and temperance if we are to achieve our goals. To exercise our concern for the expanding circle of people, we require justice. And prudence or a well-developed faculty of choice empowers us to confront life's problems.

Along with the cardinal virtues, there are a number of specific virtues under each class. Temperance divides into honor, self-control, and propriety. Prudence breaks into good judgment (as arises from knowledge of logic and physics), discretion, and resourcefulness. Justice is comprised of kindness, piety, and sociability. And courage can be divided into perseverance, magnanimity, and confidence.

The cardinal virtues, considered as wisdom, show the kind of inseparability Zeno referred to. Prudence, wisdom applied to living in a society or with others generally in your circle of concern, is justice. Endurance in work and life and in the face of fears and hardships is wisdom in the form of courage. And wisdom in choice and aversion, and in emotional attachment, is temperance. One might even go so far as to say, as Chrysippus did, that the virtues form a kind of web. For example, if I do not show wisdom in my choices, I cannot choose to endure a difficult situation. And if I am not just, if I do not show wisdom in my relationships with others, I will be intemperate in my relationships, taking too much or too little without contributing in turn.

Cicero says that justice consists in giving others what they deserve. The end of justice is, first, treating others in a way that benefits both parties involved. This is akin to honoring a contract, one whose first clause is not to do harm. Beyond the advantage of both parties, however, justice also serves and advances the ends of human society as a whole. By fulfilling our duties with regard to justice we bolster trust in cooperation between all parties involved in agreements. Opposed to justice is injustice, which Cicero, in his *On Duties*, describes as follows:

"Now the foundation of justice is faithfulness, which is a perseverance and truth in all our declarations -and in all our promises. Let us therefore (though some people may think it over nice) imitate the Stoics, who curiously examine whence terms are derived, and consider that the word faithfulness (jides), is no other than a performance of what we have premised. But there are two kinds of injustice; the first is of those who offer an injury, the second of those who have it in their power to avert an injury from those to whom it is offered, and yet do it not."[12]

Courage is also called greatness of strength or of the noble spirit. This is not what we typically consider courage to be, but it is, for the Stoics, its defining characteristic. Not only does it involve attaining those things that make our lives better, whether through hard work and discipline or through endurance, but also in rising above what we have acquired. Insofar as bettering ourselves in any way requires us to face difficulties and challenges and to rise above our present condition, it is an act of courage.

The latter aspect of rising above what we gain, orderly behavior and self-control, the Stoics call temperance. A certain amount of propriety in daily life conserves what is good tout court and what is befitting of any particular situation.

The virtues are also closely connected in structure with the three *topoi*, logic, ethics, and physics. The three *topoi* correspond to three Stoic disciplines—desire, action, and assent. Let's look briefly at each of these disciplines and how

---

[12] Cicero, *On Duties*

they tie the *topoi* to the virtues. Epictetus says of these three disciplines in his *Enchiridion*,

"The first and most necessary topic in philosophy is that of the use of moral theorems, such as, 'We ought not to lie;' the second is that of demonstrations, such as, 'What is the origin of our obligation not to lie'" the third gives strength and articulation to the other two, such as, "What is the origin of this is a demonstration.' For what is demonstration? What is consequence? What contradiction? What truth? What falsehood? The third topic, then, is necessary on the account of the second, and the second on the account of the first. But the most necessary, and that whereon we ought to rest, is the first. But we act just on the contrary. For we spend all our time on the third topic, and employ all our diligence about that, and entirely neglect the first. Therefore, at the same time that we lie, we are immediately prepared to show how it is demonstrated that lying is not right."[13]

Desire derives from physics. One must train to want only what is possible and to ignore what the universe doesn't allow. For the Stoics, this well-maintained desire is rooted in cause and effect. Through acquaintance with what the causes

---

13   Epictetus, *Enchiridion*

of circumstances and events are, one is steeled against outcomes inconsistent with what is in one's own power. Of course, extreme examples involve the desire to live forever or to live a life without suffering. But also included are desires involving other people, for them to never disappoint you or to do what is contrary to their nature or moral development. Desire is therefore linked to courage and temperance. Courage, in this case, is endurance in the face of fortune, good and bad. Temperance, in this case, is well-regulated desire. The Stoics refer to desire as the doctrine of acceptance.

Action, also called Stoic philanthropy, is the idea that humans ought to develop concern for others that is in accord with the exercise of justice. This is the discipline closest ethics. The Stoics believe that we exist for other people, to teach them and to develop with them. If we can do neither, we should at least suffer their faults, aware that they are also reflections of our own follies.

Assent is also called Stoic mindfulness. We make choices about which experiences we accept and reject. Knowing what lessons are to be drawn is related to prudence. It is therefore dependent upon logic. Assent also governs opinion. If I believe something, I am giving assent to it. But if I believe things without sufficient evidence, I am imprudent with respect to my opinions. And perhaps the most important beliefs I have concern the nature of the cosmos as a whole and my place within it.

Stoic Logic and You

We come now to a branch of Stoic philosophy not often discussed, and not discussed in great detail where it is mentioned: Stoic logic. Prudence, practical wisdom about matters great and small in ethical life, owes its power to both logic and physics, where the former studies what consequences follow from what premises and the latter supplies the premises for sound arguments. If we are to make prudent decisions, to judge when and to what extent specific actions are to be taken, we must have firm support upon which to ground and to justify our choices. Epictetus makes this point well in chapter seven, book one of his *Discourses* when he says,

"For what is the end proposed in reasoning? To establish true propositions, to remove the false, to withhold assent from those which are not plain. Is it enough then to have learned only this? "It is enough," a man may reply. Is it, then, also enough for a man, who would not make a mistake in the use of coined money, to have heard this precept, that he should receive the genuine drachmae and reject the spurious? "It is not enough." What, then, ought to be added to this precept? What else than the faculty which proves and distinguishes the genuine and the spurious drachmae?

Consequently also in reasoning what has been said is not enough; but is it necessary that a man should acquire the faculty of examining and distinguishing the true and the false, and that which is not plain? "It is necessary."[14]

In this chapter, we will discuss Stoic logic in particular, but the Stoics do not exhaust the field. As always, I encourage you to seek other sources and to study other kinds of logic if you find the coming discussion interesting or helpful.

The reasons for modern disinterest in Stoic logic are many. The field has moved far beyond the concepts available to the ancients since the development of modern logic, due in large part to Gottlob Frege and Bertrand Russell. And many modern Stoics are more interested in ethical doctrines psychological insights than the nuts and bolts of ancient Stoic cannon—with good reason. But the greatest hurdle to any engagement with Stoic logic is the scarcity of surviving works. We know, as previously mentioned, that Chrysippus alone wrote dozens of texts exploring a range of logical topics, none of which survive. What remains is gathered from a number of disparate sources, some of which contain conflicting testimonies and unreliable accounts. In the interest of

---

14 See Epictetus, *Discourses,* book one, chapter seven

providing consistent exposition, I will draw primarily from two authors: Sextus Empiricus and Diogenes Laertius. Combined, I think, they chart a robust logical theory that I hope here to make both digestible and useful for the application of Stoic ethics.

Our discussion of Stoic logic will begin with their theory of meaning or a semantic theory in modern parlance. For the Stoics, words mean what can be said in a particular language, and what can be said stands for objects in the world. To put it another way, what can be said are expressions of thoughts, and thoughts correspond to the objects about which they are thought. If I point to a particular plant and say "tree," the word signifies a thought in my head, the object of which is the observed plant. On an alternative view of meaning in Stoicism, what can be said does not correspond directly with what is thought, but derives meaning from other words which, as a complex web, are related indirectly to thought. Under this view, the sentence "that is a tree" gains its meaning from the grammatical use of the words in combination, and the combination of words has a fuzzy or imperfect relationship with the thoughts in our head. For our purposes, it is enough to assume the first theory and to not wade too deeply into this rich, but difficult, debate.

That quick detour accomplished, let us turn now to Stoic semantics. Stoic syllogisms, arguments consisting of two premises and one conclusion, are propositional, meaning that the terms involved are whole propositions. Contrast this to Aristotelian logic, often called predicate logic because its terms were subjects, that which is affirmed or denied, and predicates, that which is affirmed or denied of the subject. The most familiar Aristotelian syllogism is of the figure 1) All birds are animals. 2) All crows are birds. 3) Therefore, all crows are animals. Arguments of this kind, in which the middle term connects two universal statements, are one type of syllogism identified by Aristotle. He called it the first figure. But Aristotle's syllogism, though powerful in its own right, cannot in any figure handle arguments with complex premises like 1) If my dog is barking, the mailman has arrived. 2) My dog is barking. 3) Therefore, the mailman has arrived. Stoic logic, however, can parse arguments with complex premises.

Stoic arguments may be classified in several ways, first into valid and invalid arguments. For the Stoics, an argument is valid when the conditional (if-then) has the conjunction of its premises as its antecedent and the conclusion as its consequence, and that consequence is evaluated "true." In the previous example of my dog and the mailman, the conjoined antecedents are premises 1 and 2 and the consequence is 3. If both of the antecedents are fulfilled, then the consequence must be true, therefore the argument is valid. You are likely familiar with a version of this definition of validity already, so I will not spend too much time with it here.

Next, a valid argument is either true or not true. In a true argument, both the premises and the conclusion are evaluated true. This is best shown by an example of a not true valid argument. 1) If my dog is barking, the sun will rise. 2) My dog is barking. 3) The sun will rise. The argument is valid because if the conjunction of the antecedents hold, the conclusion must follow. But premise 1 is clearly false; my dog's barking does not always mean the sun will rise. She may just as well bark in the middle of the night. Though the argument is valid, then, it is not true. This is also likely familiar to you already. Today we call this the distinction between a sound and an unsound argument.

True valid arguments may be demonstrative or not demonstrative. Demonstrative arguments show something new or not-evident from premises that are already recognized to be the case or that are evident. For an example of this kind of argument, I will turn to Sextus Empiricus' Outlines of Pyrrhonism. There he says "1) If sweat flows through the surface of the skin, there exist imperceptible pores. 2) Sweat flows through the surface of the skin. 3) Therefore, there exist imperceptible pores." These are the kinds of arguments we often see in the disciplines, whether they be in the sciences or the humanities. If an argument does not yield a novel conclusion, then it is not demonstrative. The Stoics also recognize undemonstrated arguments, which purport to yield new information but have not yet been proven. We might think of these as untested hypotheses, or as arguments in a greater chain of reasoning whose demonstration depends on the conclusion of that chain. They are not to be confused with not demonstrative arguments which yield no new information. At this point note that whether an argument is undemonstrated or demonstrated may vary with respect to time. This temporality is a curious feature of Stoic logic to which we will return later.

Demonstrated true valid arguments may proceed through memory and belief alone toward their conclusion or may proceed through memory and belief and discovery. I will again turn to Sextus Empiricus for an example of an argument whose conclusion is reached through memory and belief alone. Again in Outlines of Pyrrhonism, he says "1) If someone said to you that this man would be wealthy, this man will be wealthy. 2) This god said to you that this man would be wealthy. 3) Therefore, this man will be wealthy." Sextus says that assent to the conclusion of this argument depends on the belief in the god and in the god's assertion. There is an example closer in structure and assumption to our own time I think we can use. 1) If an official says the war would go well, the war will go well. 2) The president says the war would go well. 3) The war will go well. Assent to this argument depends not upon the necessity of its premises, but upon our trust in the current president. Of those demonstrated arguments requiring both memory or belief and discovery, Sextus' pore example is an instance. We require an assumption or belief that moisture does not flow through solid bodies.

Undemonstrated arguments have two forms, those which may be demonstrated in time as mentioned above and those which are non-temporal. Those undemonstrated arguments that are non-temporal are referred to as "inference schemata." There are five such non-temporal undemonstrated arguments into whose forms all other true and valid arguments in Stoic logic fall. We will take a brief look at each of them now and then move on to applications of Stoic logic in Stoic ethics.

The first non-temporal undemonstrated is today known as modus ponendo ponens. It is the form of argument we have, to this point, been using in our examples. If p, then q; p; therefore, q. As we've seen, this schemata has a conditional and its antecedent as premises, followed by the consequent of the conditional as its conclusion. As Epictetus says in book two, chapter six of his *Discourses*,

"The hypothetical proposition is indifferent: the judgment about it is not indifferent, but it is either knowledge or opinion or error. Thus life is indifferent: the use is not indifferent. When any man then tells you that these things also are indifferent, do not become negligent; and when a man invites you to be careful, do not become abject and struck with admiration of material things. And it is good for you to know your own preparation and power, that in those matters where you have not been prepared, you may keep quiet, and not be vexed if others have the advantage over you. For you, too, in syllogisms will claim to have the advantage over them; and if others should be vexed at this, you will console them by saying, "I have learned them, and you have not." Thus also where there is need of any practice, seek not that which is required for the need, but yield in that matter to those who have had practice, and be yourself content with firmness of mind."[15]

The second schemata is today known as modus tollendo tollens. Its form is as follows: If p, then q; not q; therefore, not-p. For this schemata, the conditional and the contradiction of its consequence as premises. From that, the contradiction of the antecedent follows as the conclusion. I will provide a brief example. 1) If I am going to the car wash, then my car will be cleaned. 2) My car will not be cleaned (or not-my car will be cleaned. 2) Therefore, I am not going to the car wash (or not-I am going to the car wash).

The third schemata is nameless, but it should nonetheless be familiar. Its form is: Not p and q; p; therefore, not-q. We may phrase this as "not both" p and q. So, for example, 1) Not both x is good and x is evil. 2) x is good. 3) Therefore, not x is evil. In this schemata a negative conjunction is the premise along with one of its conjuncts (so p and q, and p respectively in this case). The necessary conclusion, then, is the contradiction of the remaining conjunct.

Schemata four is today called modus ponendo tollens. Its form is as follows: Either p or q; p; therefore, not-q. For

---

[15] Epictetus, *Discourses,* book two, chapter six

example, 1) Either I will go to college or I will work in my parents' bakery. 2) I will work in my parents' bakery. 3) Therefore, I will not go to college (or not-I will go to college). In this schemata a disjunction and one of its disjuncts are premises. The conclusion then is the contradiction of the remaining disjunct.

Finally, schemata five is today known as modus tollendo ponens. Either p or q; not-q; therefore, p. For example, 1) Either I will go to college or I will work in my parents' bakery. 2) I will not work in my parents' bakery (or not-I will work in my parents' bakery). 3) Therefore, I will go to college. In this schemata the disjunct and the contradiction of one of its disjuncts are premises. It follows, then, that the other disjunct is the conclusion.

Logic as an aid to Stoic teachings serve our inner life, that we do not live in a cloud of confusion in matters of right and wrong, and that we do not thereby choose vice instead of virtue. Epictetus gives a number of examples and deploys metaphor in describing the importance of sound arguments. We can explore more contemporary examples. If a friend tells me that my time with them is too short, that I am abusive because of my inattention, and thereby concludes that I am either actively malicious or at least indifferent to their feelings, might we consider this an argument of the fourth or the fifth schemata? If the fifth, my friend is saying that I am either indifferent or malicious. If I deny my intentions are malicious, they will call me indifferent instead, justifying their ire. If I want to avoid this trap, I should deny their original disjunction as false by asserting a third option into their dilemma.

That example was simple enough, what about a more difficult one? Say I am dealing with a difficult colleague. After requesting she complete a task for me, she tells me that she will be away for the weekend. Do I lose my temper with her? In the case that I do, my reasoning could be something like this: I can't both keep a level head and avoid being trampled on and disrespected by her. Superficially this choice seems to match the form of schema three; not-I can keep a level head and keep my dignity. But we can reveal the deceptiveness of this dilemma via the first two schemata. For example, the inference "if I do not lose my temper, then I will be disrespected" can be proven false by considering whether or not it has been demonstrated in the past. Is it true that in all cases where I do not lose my temper I am disrespected, or is there another way I can express myself? Similarly, the implication "If I lose my temper, I will be respected" can be reflected on. Does a short fuse lead to respect in every circumstance? Does it lead to respect in any circumstance? The Stoics would say no, but I leave it to you to decide. When you do so, remember the difference between respect and intimidation.

There are a number of other examples I could introduce, but lived experience and active reflection are, I think, the best ways to learn Stoic rules of inference and Stoic logic. We are not quite done with these rules; we will see them again in all the following chapters indirectly, and in more explicit form when discussing some of the logical pitfalls identified by cognitive behavioral therapy and more immediately in thinking about Stoicism in its relationship with theology.

Cosmology and Theology in Stoicism

Stoic ethics is incomplete without a discussion of the Divine Fire. In ethics, philosophers concern themselves with what it means to be moral, what moral living consists of, and the status of moral knowledge. But no less important to them is the question "why be moral?" Living a morally upright life, being a "moral saint" as contemporary philosopher Susan Wolf describes it, is often more difficult than living a viscous, immoral life. Part of the Stoic answer to this question is that virtue is human nature. Under this account, it is for our own benefit that we pursue virtue, so that we can achieve those ends which nature has given us, whether socially, psychologically, or spiritually. But this is only half of the Stoic response to the "why be moral?" question. Reason two is that the life in accordance with nature brings us into harmony with the will of the cosmos, the Divine Fire. As Epictetus says in his *Enchiridion*,

"Be assured that the essential property of piety towards the gods is to form right opinions concerning them, as existing "I and as governing the universe with goodness and justice. And fix yourself in this resolution, to obey them, and yield to them, and willingly follow them in all events, as produced by a perfect understanding. For thus you will never find fault with the gods, nor accuse them of neglecting you."[16]

The extent to which Divine Fire is essential to Stoicism is a matter for debate among modern Stoics. I will not wade waist deep into that argument. Divine Fire is, at its heart, a pantheist idea. It portrays the entire universe, the all, as in some way infused with divinity. But I don't think it is foreign to us in the west in particular, and to many world religions in general. We might recognize parts of Stoic pantheism in Deism, in which reason and observation are sufficient to discover God's will. To the extent that Divine Fire rejects revealed religion, we can say it is incompatible with most strains of Christianity, Hinduism, Islam, and Judaism. But I do not, for that reason alone, think Divine Fire in any way threatens the major religions of our time. And, at any rate, I do not think it is necessary to assent to or deny this Stoic doctrine to understand its place in Stoic ethics.

The "all" for the Stoics has the character of a sphere. This great copula encloses everything that is, and in it all forces, inward and outward, are balanced. Stoicism, taken as a whole, is meant to mirror this balance; it is meant to enclose and

---

[16] Epictetus, *Enchiridion*

relate all aspects of conscious experience. To that extent, Stoicism includes both reason and logic and the natural sciences on the one hand, and faith on the other. These two sides—I'll call them reason and faith for brevity, though I don't mean to imply that they are really opposed—are united by and in cosmology for the Stoics. In Stoic cosmology, the universe was born from and is driven by Divine Fire.

There are two sides to Divine Fire, the passive and active principles. The passive principle is matter without purpose. We might think of this as non-living objects, though they are, at best, the outward manifestations of this principle. Taken generally, it is that in the universe which is acted upon but does not itself act. The active principle may be thought of as the organizing principle or the law of attraction. It is what causes the passive principle to manifest as all those things in the universe which we recognize. We might also refer to the active principle as the consciousness of the universe. We, of course, recognize the outward form of this consciousness in living creatures. The Stoics say that we, as with all living creatures, are sparks of this second aspect of Divine Fire. As Marcus Aurelius says in book four of his *Meditations*,

"Constantly regard the universe as one living being, having one substance and one soul; and observe how all things have reference to one perception, the perception of this one living being; and how all things act with one movement; and how all things are the cooperating causes of all things which exist; observe too the continuous spinning of the thread and the texture of the web."[17]

Living in accordance with nature is the aim of Stoic philosophy because by doing so we live out our existence as sparks of divinity. If we do not follow this maxim, we not only harm ourselves, we harm the whole of existence. If we follow only our own interests, we introduce disharmony. Divine Fire, then, is a kind of Divine Command Theory—we follow the moral law because the Divine commands it. Further, what benefits the whole also benefits us. This idea, that we serve the whole first and thereby serve ourselves turns the idea that by following the moral law we serve ourselves on its head. Whereas the latter is a kind of egoism, says that ultimately self-development is what matters, the doctrine of Divine Fire says that ultimately the whole is what matters, and serving our own interests is a pleasant side effect. We are passive insofar as we follow this maxim, but active insofar as we, possessed of the divine spark, decide the very universal maxim we follow. We must be prepared to and

---

17   Marcus Aurelius, *Meditations,* book four

may be called to, sacrifice our own interests if thereby a greater, moral purpose is served.

This idea of self-sacrifice as fallen into disrepute in the 21st century, and for good reason. Both countries and religions have called on individuals to give up their particular interests for a universal value, whether it be nation or dogma. But we should divorce these (I think incorrect) calls for self-effacement from the kind of sacrifice championed in religion, meaningful political activity, and in Stoic doctrine. Whereas the former reduces the individual to parts of a greater project, the latter situate the project firmly in the individuals themselves. In Christianity, Christ lives in His subjects; in democracy, the free citizen is preserved in individual activity; in Stoicism, the Divine Fire expresses itself in moral agents. Sacrifice in extreme circumstances may involve suffering, but the foundation of that sacrifice is the conflict in each person between their particular interests and the projects they choose and enact. Rather than being irrelevant to the project, rather than being dispensable, we are first indispensable if the project is to be made manifest and second responsible for deciding what that project is. This is more in line with Stoic teachings than either nationalism or wars for religion.

STOICISM AND PSYCHOLOGY

Cognitive Behavioral Therapy, or CBT for short, is an innovative approach to psychotherapy that has flourished in the last several decades. Through the NHS, the British government has dedicated hundreds of millions to training and equipping psychologists in and with its techniques. Its founders, Albert Ellis and Aaron Beck, drew heavily from the Stoic and Socratic traditions in developing a holistic therapy, the aim of which is self-evaluation. Through this approach, the analysand is encouraged to bring their unconscious beliefs to the forefront, to address and defeat those beliefs which contribute to their illness.

Its creators stripped CBT of ethics, values, and any mention of a higher purpose or meaning and gave the ancient teachings that inspired it a scientific basis. In doing so, however, they stripped away the center of these teachings, reducing them to, at best, empirically founded self-help guides. In opposition to this approach, new schools of CBT have arisen. They include Acceptance and Commitment Therapy, positive psychology, and mindfulness-CBT. They include questions of value in therapy, and thereby involve a more robust concept of the human subject in their tool-box approach to cognitive renewal.

In his book, The Philosophy of CBT, Donald Robertson traces the roots of this modern therapeutic practice back to the ancient Greeks and Romans. For him, drawing on the comportment of the ancients, philosophy, and therapy are not entirely distinct. Ancient philosophy studied the "art of living," changing the philosopher's attitudes to alter and improve their lives. This is different from the interests of psychotherapists, whose preoccupation is health, and specifically mental health. Nonetheless, philosophers and therapists can still learn much from each other. Philosophers can gain ideas for the practical application of philosophical study, and therapists can learn concepts, strategies, and techniques that are consistent with modern models of therapy, though largely neglected.

The aim of drawing out the link between CBT and philosophy is to clarify concept and value-based issues, to strengthen psychological changes made by the former and include the reflective approach of the latter. Philosophical counseling integrated into cognitive behavioral therapy employs concepts like human flourishing, resilience, and the good life, advocating both particular healing, addressing individual and long-term problems, and lifetime results and self-reliance, integrating its lessons into a schema or framework for living well.

CBT employs an onion model of the mind. Thoughts we have, positive or negative, are usually signs of underlying beliefs. If you experience social anxiety, for example, you might believe that other people are judgmental or don't like you, or that you yourself are unlikable. These thoughts, in turn, influence your behavior. You might shy away from others or going out entirely to avoid confirming your fears. This becomes a viscous cycle; negative thoughts and emotions are reinforced by your actions, which in turn influence your thoughts and emotions. CBT aims to disrupt this cycle by analysis. Similarly, Epictetus treats anxiety as related to the doctrine of control when in chapter 13, book two of his *Discourses* he says,

"When I see a man anxious, I say, "What does this man want? If he did not want something which is not in his power, how could he be anxious?" For this reason a lute player when he is singing by himself has no anxiety, but when he enters the theatre, he is anxious even if he has a good voice and plays well on the lute; for he not only wishes to sing well but also to obtain   applause: but this is not in his power. Accordingly, where he has a skill, there he has confidence. Bring any single person who knows nothing of music, and the musician does not care for him. But on the matter where a man knows nothing and has not been practiced, there he is anxious."[18]

Through behavioral experiments, you can change your thoughts and improve your lifestyle. You can take your fears head-on and reassess the beliefs which fuel them. At the same time, you learn about human psychology, and about the mechanisms by which negative thoughts are reinforced.

CBT aims to correct those errors in thinking which lead to emotional disturbances. The literature on the topic includes a list of the errors which typically lead to harmful, self-destructive thinking. The analysand is taught to be on guard for those automatic thoughts that create negative ideas and emotions. The aim is to, when in any kind of emotional distress, confront the disruptive, core beliefs that lie a layer deeper. Though I can't here exhaust the therapeutic methods employed by cognitive behavioral therapy, I will touch on some common errors pointed out in the literature. This attitude is present in the Stoics, too. For example, when Epictetus in his *Enchiridion* says,

"Does anyone bathe in a mighty little time? Don't say that he does it ill, but in a mighty little time. Does anyone drink a

---

[18]   Epictetus, *Discourses,* book two, chapter thirteen

great quantity of wine? Don't say that he does ill, but that he drinks a great quantity. For, unless you perfectly understand the principle from which anyone acts, how should you know if he acts ill? Thus you will not run the hazard of assenting to any appearances but such as you fully comprehend."[19]

The principle of thinking through our disturbances exemplified here is at the hear of the CBT method of therapy.

One common error is the overgeneralization. The core of this error is a kind of hyperbole. When some negative event happens, or some perceived personality or behavioral defect appears, the person experiencing it tends to think that it happens all the time, or that the flaw is in some way essential to them as a person. If, for example, I'm in a situation where I make some social gaffe or slight someone unintentionally, I might deride myself as socially inept or antisocial. And if I fail to complete a task, or fail to complete one well, I might call myself incompetent or stupid, turning a temporary error into just another example of my ineptitude.

Another error is in the attribution of blame. In some cases, one might take any criticism or negative remark as a comment about their own worth. Alternately, in the same vein,

---

19   Epictetus, *Enchiridion*

accidents of fortune or mistakes others have made are personalized. If for example, someone tells me my presentation could use work or is below expectation, I am making a mistake if I tie my own worth to the success of a single project. Or if my computer stops working or some critical software has a bug or a virus, I might scold myself for not taking better care of it, or for not backing up my files when I had the chance. The other half of this error is taking too little blame or blaming others. If my truck stops working while an employee has it, it would be incorrect for me to blame the employee if it is my responsibility to change the battery, to ensure the vehicle is in good condition.

Black and white thinking is a third kind of error referred to in the literature. This is another way we might exaggerate a situation, good or bad. If I did poorly on an exam, for instance, I might say I have completely blown my chances for a good grade. On the other hand, if I do well, I might become lax, thinking I've overcome the greatest hurdle the class has to offer.

A common error in our thinking, related to over generalizing, is jumping to conclusions. Is there sufficient evidence for me to believe something about the future? If I, before going to a party, say to myself that I will be an embarrassment or a "drag" socially, am I really justified in saying that? Or, if someone else gives me a sly look or a look I find insulting, is it right for me to jump to the conclusion that they don't like me or that they are plotting against me? Often these mistakes occur because of bad experiences in the past. But are these experiences reason to think the present or the future holds the same pitfalls?

CBT also warns us against incorrectly moralizing a situation. Good and bad only apply to actions and choices, as we've seen in the chapter on Stoic morality. So if I, after experiencing some misfortune outside of my control, say that it should or ought to have gone another way, I am mistaken in externalizing a moral imperative. There is no particular way that an event outside of my control should or ought to have gone. Only my actions and my disposition toward fortune should be some way or another. Of those things over which I have no control, I can declare no obligation for them to produce one result or another.

The last error we'll look at is the error of mental filtering. This error involves selective sight of either positive or negative events. Alternatively, we might notice when something nice happens to us, but value it less than negative events. If someone compliments me for an accomplishment, I might dismiss them as just being nice, or even twist their complement into a slight. "You did well on this exam" can become "you haven't done well on the others," or "you did well, but I did better."

CBT uses a variety of techniques to address these and other errors. We start by pointing out the error, then we examine and criticize it. First, we ask ourselves what error applies to the negative thought or emotion we are experiencing. Then we look at the facts of the matter. Is there evidence for what we're feeling? Is there evidence against it? The facts become weights or reasons by which we can judge our thinking correct or incorrect.

After the thought has been examined in detail, the next step is to be both honest and sympathetic with ourselves. CBT calls us not to use double standards. Instead of being tough on ourselves, of talking down to ourselves about what errors we make, we should treat ourselves as we would a good friend. We don't hide the mistakes we make; the point of searching for the errors was, in the first place, in the service of honesty. But we also should not be flippant toward our negative emotions, nor should we seek to tear ourselves down over what may be honest mistakes in our thinking.

Next, we are warned against "all or nothing" thinking. Think, instead, of a continuum in which you, like most other people, fall somewhere between the extremes. If I did poorly on an exam, I should think that I've lost several percentage points in my overall grade, not that I have blown the class entirely. Or if someone appears disappointed in my behavior or performance, I should think that I have upset them in this instance, not that our relationship is over.

It is important to avoid emotionally front-loading ourselves. Instead, we should use descriptive language when assessing our situations. Instead of saying "I'm a disappointment," say "I could have done better here." Where you might say "this is the worst possible outcome," say "this could have gone better in certain respects." The goal is to express facts instead of feeling, to describe and analyze the situation instead of reacting to it. As Marcus Aurelius ponders in book twelve of his *Meditations*,

"I have often wondered how it is that every man loves himself more than all the rest of men, but yet sets less value on his own opinion of himself than on the opinion of others. If then a god or a wise teacher should present himself to a man and bid him to think of nothing and to design nothing which he would not express as soon as he conceived it, he could not endure it even for a single day. So much more respect have we to what our neighbors shall think of us than to what we shall think of ourselves."[20]

We should also examine the consequences of what we feel and do, both in the short and long term. There are pros and cons to everything we engage in. What are they? Does it serve us to lose our temper? What about denigrating ourselves? And if so, to what degree? We'll see later that the Stoics think it is never right to lose one's temper. Will you behave more rationally if you are emotionally excited? How might that affect other people or your own dispositions?

Finally, when should "should" and "ought" be used? Is an action commended or denounced in the power of you or another person? If not, they should be avoided. Further, if you or another person have some obligation, is there a conflicting obligation that overrides it? Maybe, in the case of other people, they weigh value differently than you. Is what you or they ought to do a universal value, or is it a cultural, societal, or religious preference? As Emperor Marcus Aurelius says in his *Meditations* book seven,

---

[20] Marcus Aurelius, *Meditations*, book twelve

"When a man has done thee any wrong, immediately consider with what opinion about good or evil he has done wrong. For when thou hast seen this, thou wilt pity him, and wilt neither wonder nor be angry. For either thou thyself thinkest the same thing to be good that he does or another thing of the same kind. It is thy duty then to pardon him. But if thou dost not think such things to be good or evil, thou wilt more readily be well disposed to him who is in error."[21]

This is not to say that there aren't universal values, or that right and wrong are relative, but that there are situations in which we confuse concrete duties with personal or group opinion. If you understand your own values and the values of others against the background of encompassing ethical theories, you may find that what you or they "should" do is really a matter of divergent moral premises.

Philosophical CBT, of course, extends well beyond what I've said here, with a wealth of specialized techniques and diagnosis, but I hope to have adequately covered the basics. If you have a particular problem, a pattern of reoccurring thoughts or behaviors, seeking a specialist in cognitive behavioral therapy will provide a wealth of tools with which

---

[21] Marcus Aurelius, *Meditations,* book seven

to address them. And incorporating treatment with a Stoic mindset, introducing a new attitude toward life as a whole, can be a robust and long-lasting solution. You don't have to fight this battle alone.

Stoicism and the Emotions

It is no coincidence that cognitive behavioral therapy, inspired by ancient philosophy, puts a lot of emphasis on our emotional responses. Stoicism in general, and especially the doctrine of control, views our responses as central to human flourishing. But it is a mistake to think the Stoics, true to our modern use of their name, are resigned or emotionless. A Stoic disposition requires mastery over one's emotions, not abandonment. In this chapter, we'll take a look at what emotional mastery entails, how we fall short, and what Stoicism can teach us about emotional temperance.

Epictetus in his Discourses says Stoics are trained to act virtuously through the concepts of "appropriate action" and "discipline of action." Appropriate action concerns what we choose and avoid in our familial and social interactions. Discipline of action concerns what we choose and avoid in ourselves, what desires and habits we allow ourselves to cultivate. Both require emotional attachment to some extent, whether for others or for ourselves. Both also require that these attachments are grounded in good judgment. Stoics, ancient and modern, think that affection for one's close friends and family, for one's country, and for the whole of humanity, is natural. This expanded sphere of concern, and our resulting social wealth protect us from becoming too attached to one person or a few people. We can accept these emotions while remembering that those we care for may not live up to our expectations, that they may disappoint us. What others do is outside of our control, but we need not for that reason be indifferent to their well-being.

There is a difference between apatheia (Stoic resilience) and insensitivity. The former means one is not vulnerable to their emotions. They do not rule over us. Cicero says that the latter, insensitivity or lacking all emotion, is among the most debased ways of living. Even animals exhibit kinship and emotional attachment. By eschewing all attachment, not only are we not living up to our nature as humans, we are below animals. He says that in such a state we are more akin to a tree or a rock. Seneca further says that there can be no virtue for someone like this. To be courageous, to have self-discipline, one needs to exercise fortitude. But there is no fortitude if the challenge one is confronted with is in no way difficult. Ridding oneself of all emotions is not mastery of emotions. If feeling were to return, the insensitive person would in no way be prepared, would not have the judgment or the habits needed to overcome them. They were never confronted by an obstacle whose overcoming strengthened them, were never in a rough patch by which they could develop calluses.

Cognitive Behavioral Therapy inherited its diagnosis of the source of unhealthy emotions from Stoicism. In Stoicism, these emotions are created by irrational responses to adversity, whether overvaluing what is not in our control or desiring what is not possible. The goal is not to distance yourself from your emotions, but to identify their sources, the beliefs upon which they are founded, and replace them with new, healthy beliefs.

In Stoicism, there are also both healthy and unhealthy negative emotions. Negative in this context does not mean bad, but unpleasant, sad, or painful. Healthy negative emotions motivate us to make a change, to pursue virtue or to alter our perceptions. At the very least, they push us to avoid outcomes that could otherwise debilitate us. In place of anxiety, an unhealthy negative emotion, we might experience concern or worry. Sadness, grief, and mourning are all healthy and, opposed to depression, motivate us to overcome our circumstances or put what we have lost to rest psychologically.

Anger has a special place in the Stoic cannon. Unlike sadness or fear, anger is never permissible for the Stoics. The Stoics think that there are three components to anger. First, the perception of being wronged. This might happen when someone talks down to you, ignores you, insults you, or in any other way diminishes you. The second component is the feeling that the wrong is undeserved. If someone talks down to me or slights me after I've messed up, I might be more inclined to feel guilty or sad unless I somehow twist their words or actions so they appear to me to be uncalled for. Finally, the angry person must have the desire to retaliate. In other words, I want to "balance" the scales, to get back at them, to diminish them in kind and bring them down to my level.

We should guard ourselves especially against adopting the anger of others. If someone is angry with you, if they're attacking you verbally, giving you the cold shoulder, or defaming you in the presence of others, you may very well become angry in turn. Remember Epictetus' words from his *Enchiridion*,

"When any person harms you, or speaks badly of you, remember that he acts or speaks from a supposition of its being his duty. Now, it is not possible that he should follow what appears right to you, but what appears so to himself. Therefore, if he judges from a wrong appearance, he is the person hurt, since he too is the person deceived. For if anyone should suppose a true proposition to be false, the proposition is not hurt, but he who is deceived about it. Setting out, then, from these principles, you will meekly bear a person who reviles you, for you will say upon every occasion, 'It seemed so to him.'"[22]

In this case, you might think you're justified. After all, the other person injured themselves; they did not show patience in dealing with you, so why should you be patient with them? This kind of emotional spillover—from another person—is all too common in relationships and work environments. But is it really sound to argue that they deserve to suffer in the same way they're causing you to suffer?

Epictetus says that there is never a cause to get angry. The only way another person could "injure" us is by attacking or debasing some external, whether it be our property, our bodies, or our reputation. But none of these are really ours, we do not control them. What we do control is our internal lives, our faculty of choice, and it is that very faculty that is injured when we lose our temper. By getting angry, we skew our judgment and sacrifice our discipline. This kind of debasement is not something any other person or any external circumstance can do to us. We bring this upon ourselves.

---

22   Epictetus, *Enchiridion*

Anger tends toward a kind of mission creep. When angry, we often misjudge what is and isn't in our control. First, we misjudge whether or not the source of our anger really injured us, whether it in any way diminished our inner lives. Second, we misjudge whether or not becoming angry will harm the object of our anger, whether person or thing. Outwardly, we can insult them or damage their person or property, but they themselves can only be harmed if they allow it. Even in this latter case, it is never we ourselves who are doing the harm.

The discussion of anger brings us back around to the preferred Stoic method of combating emotional malfeasance, shifting perspective. In this case, is what we're angry about really under our control? If my friend goes a few weeks without talking to me, but it's clear that they're still talking to others, that is their choice, painful though it might be for me. Instead of lessening the pain their indifference causes me, I'm only adding to it by seething, by dwelling on their actions. And if I decide to curse them out, to yell, to make a scene, is it more or less likely that they will want to remain friends? I must show discipline (*ascesis*) and endure their actions, remembering that they are also free subjects, capable of making decisions with regard to their inner and outer life, even if their actions disappoint me.

What is the Stoic approach to fear, and how can we master our fears using Stoic methods? The Stoics identify two types of fears. The fist kind is a knee-jerk response to certain stimuli, like being startled or disgusted by an unexpected event or sensation. The ancient Stoics called this *propatheia*, pre-emotions. They are often physiological responses, as unmediated as one blocking his or her face when a ball is thrown at it. It is after we experience these surprises that we judge their cause positive or negative, good or bad. If, after experiencing and reflecting upon it, we judge that the thing responsible is a true evil or harm, we experience real fear.

The Stoics emphasize that real fear is a choice or a judgment we consciously make. It is up to us whether we assert or deny that a thing is truly frightening, and further how to respond to it. If we do not assent that a thing is frightening or threatening, we will not be afraid. The Stoics do not, therefore, suggest that we eschew all fears, that we become totally fearless or insensible to danger. Rather, the Stoics recommend we replace fear with caution, *eulabeia*. This state does not combine worry and anxiety with fear, but instead with conscientiousness and curiosity. Instead of being shuttered away from our fears, we are called to become intimate with them, too, through a thorough acquaintance with their origins and functioning, master them. Rather than a disposition open to recklessness, the Stoic response is informed resignation, such that we accept our fears to defeat them.

To conclude our discussion of the emotions, before moving on to Stoic exercises, consider what it means to master them. Grief, anger, and anxiety tend to, when unrestrained, become habits. We can feel restrained and even helpless when we eschew them. If someone diminishes me and I don't retaliate, I may feel that I'm being trampled upon. If I do not express my sadness at some loss, if I do not let myself go, I can feel bottled up, repressed. Remember the words of Marcus Aurelius from book twelve of his *Meditations*:

"When thou art troubled about anything, thou hast forgotten this, that all things happen according to the universal nature; and forgotten this, that a man's wrongful act is nothing to thee; and further thou hast forgotten this, that everything which happens, always happened so and will happen so, and now happens so everywhere; forgotten this too, how close is the kinship between a man and the whole human race, for it is a community, not of a little blood or seed, but of intelligence. And thou hast forgotten this too, that every man's intelligence is a god, and is an efflux of the deity; and forgotten this, that nothing is a man's own, but that his child and his body and his very soul came from the deity; forgotten this, that everything is opinion; and lastly thou hast forgotten that every man lives the present time only, and loses only this." [23]

To a certain extent, these are correct interpretations. But consider that restrained grief, grief that is healthy and directed toward some end, is more productive toward healing than a spiral into depression. Similarly, anger spirals out of control. It is like a fire that consumes everything, both its object and us. It is more productive toward proving that we are not as small as fate or another person would have us feel to hold our temper, to rise above subservience to passion. In both cases, retaining our judgment secures our needs better than our emotional response. Think of the words of Emperor Marcus Aurelius, from book five of his *Meditations*,

"Art thou angry with him whose armpits stink? Art thou angry with him whose mouth smells foul? What good will this danger do thee? He has such a mouth, he has such armpits: it is necessary that such an emanation must come from such things- but the man has reason, it will be said, and he is able, if he takes pain, to discover wherein he offends- I wish thee well of thy discovery."[24]

---

23 Marcus Aurelius, *Meditations,* book twelve
24 Marcus Aurelius, *Meditations,* book five

A life of emotional mastery is no more unrestrained than it is insensible. It is in this mean between the extremes, in addressing what we feel rationally, that we satisfy those aims which our emotions demand. This is a life of engaged contentment, the core of which vigilance and exercise.

Outer Troubles; Preventative Measures in Stoicism

What we choose and what we avoid says a lot about who we are. It broadcasts our priorities, whether concerning which people we prefer, or which objects. It also determines when our quality of life will be disrupted. If we attach ourselves to the wrong things, to externals, positive or negative, we open ourselves to suffering and misfortune. A key Stoic concept is, therefore, to steel oneself against negative circumstances, to win the battle for our inner life before it's fought. This chapter focuses on preventive Stoic exercises, those actions you can take before you're faced with a dilemma. We will examine the methods and the mental states, many over two thousand years old, that great Stoics like Epictetus, Marcus Aurelius, Seneca, and Musonius Rufus taught and used, and, through example, apply these circumstances to modern life.

Marcus Aurelius championed a technique today referred to as "the view from above." Therein he recommended a kind of withdrawn attitude toward your circumstances, one that views particular events in relation to the whole of creation. We should strive, Marcus thinks, to rid ourselves of those useless things which disturb us. If we see how rapidly the world changes, how short the individual's life is and how vast the passage of time was before we were born and will be after we die, we can protect ourselves from trifles before they occur.

The view from above is partly related to the doctrine of control discussed in an earlier chapter. The aim of both is to fix in our minds those things worth our concern. What should I fear from death? Is it not the case that every person before has died, and that every person will die, and that eventually, the whole human race will be extinct? I'll let Marcus speak for himself. In book two of his *Meditations*, he says,

"Every moment think steadily as a Roman and a man to do what thou hast in hand with perfect and simple dignity, and feeling of affection, and freedom, and justice; and to give thyself relief from all other thoughts. And thou wilt give thyself relief, if thou doest every act of thy life as if it were the last, laying aside all carelessness and passionate aversion from the commands of reason, and all hypocrisy, and self-love, and discontent with the portion which has been given to thee. Thou seest how few the things are, the which if a man lays hold of, he is able to live a life which flows in quiet, and is like the existence of the gods; for the gods on their part will require nothing more from him who observes these things."[25]

My suffering, then, and my fear of death, is minuscule when considered in relation to the whole of existence. Marcus challenges us to take this view toward death so we can live with purpose. If even my death is a minuscule event, how much smaller is that irritation I felt in the office last week? Was it worth dwelling on for days?

When we get up in the morning, Marcus says, we should remember exactly how small we are. Remember that we will have to face people no less small, to suffer any number of indignities, and to conduct ourselves with poise. In book two of his *Meditations*, Marcus says,

"Begin the morning by saying to thyself, I shall meet with the busy-body, the ungrateful, arrogant, deceitful, envious, unsocial. All these things happen to them by reason of their ignorance of what is good and evil. But I who have seen the nature of the good that it is beautiful, and of the bad that it is ugly, and the nature of him who does wrong, that it is akin to me, not only of the same blood or seed, but that it participates in the same intelligence and the same portion of the divinity, I

---

25 Marcus Aurelius, *Meditations*, book two

can neither be injured by any of them, for no one can fix on me what is ugly, nor can I be angry with my kinsman, nor hate him, For we are made for co-operation, like feet, like hands, like eyelids, like the rows of the upper and lower teeth. To act against one another then is contrary to nature; and it is acting against one another to be vexed and to turn away."[26]

If we keep in mind that those who vex us face the same fate we do, we can accept whatever minor victory they perceive for themselves when they diminish us. Even the highest, most powerful people cannot escape death, they will also be swept aside in the long-run. It, therefore, matters even less to what degree someone's pettiness elevates them. They are not as important as great people, and even great people are not important at all. Marcus Aurelius counsels us about such people when he says:

"Besides wherein hast thou been injured? For thou wilt find that no one among those against whom thou art irritated has done anything by which thy mind could be made worse; but that which is evil to thee and harmful has its foundation only in the mind. And what harm is done or what is there strange, if the man who has not been instructed does the acts of an

---

26   Marcus Aurelius, *Meditations,* book two

uninstructed man? Consider whether thou shouldst not rather blame thyself, because thou didst not expect such a man to err in such a way. For thou hadst means given thee by thy reason to suppose that it was likely that he would commit this error, and yet thou hast forgotten and art amazed that he has erred."[27]

There is another technique whose center is a recognition of our finitude. Seneca says that it is important to love the people in our circle, but we must remember that they are not ours to keep. Fate brought them into our lives, and fate will eventually take them from us. We must, therefore, while loving them, remember that they will not always be with us. We must practice our love for them such that we take full advantage of our limited time together. This exercise is double-edged: First we should take joy and comfort in them where we can, second, we should limit our enjoyment, not become singularly attached or fixated on spending time with them.

How does this look in practice? My grandmother is very old now. In comparison to me, her time is short. But what time she does have she dedicates to us, to her family. Not a day

---

[27] ibid

goes by where she isn't visited by at least one of us, and often it's several of us together. This is the kind of behavior about which Seneca speaks. We should treat all those we care about as though their time is short because it is. In doing so we not only maximize what little time we have, we also prepare for the end of that time.

Another kind of exercise, also recommended by Marcus Aurelius, is premeditating evil. Imagine the worst that can happen during your day, your year, or your lifetime. Imagine yourself stricken with poverty or illness, or imagine that your endeavors fail. What do these misfortunes feel like? What will you do to confront them? Marcus says we should move our minds toward overcoming them; we should imagine ourselves enduring disappointments and setbacks, and then growing in spite of them. We should also imagine ourselves shifting our focus back toward the good, toward virtue, while wrapped in despair. As Marcus says in book four of his *Meditations*,

"Men seek retreats for themselves, houses in the country, seashores, and mountains; and thou too art wont to desire such things very much. But this is altogether a mark of the most common sort of men, for it is in thy power whenever thou shalt choose to retire into thyself. For nowhere either with more quiet or more freedom from trouble does a man retire than into his own soul, particularly when he has within him such thoughts that by looking into them he is immediately in perfect tranquility; and I affirm that tranquillity is nothing else than the good ordering of the mind."[28]

We might draw an analogy to physical exercise here. Some people find it helpful to, before a workout, visualize what the workout will involve, the discomfort they'll experience, and their desire to quit half-way, to prepare themselves mentally. They also imagine the end of the workout and what benefits they'll reap after their routine is over. When the time comes to start the routine, they've already prepped themselves for the strain, they have anticipated every aspect of their training, including the desire to quit. What Marcus recommends is also the anticipation of a strenuous workout, but for the mind and for our willpower. This is another good exercise to try early in the morning, before work or school, especially when you anticipate less than pleasant people. Imagine your goal, whether it be passing the class, receiving your paycheck, or just making it home afterward.

---

28   Marcus Aurelius, *Meditations*, book four

Related to this defensive technique is the exercise of writing Stoic aphorisms. When you start your day, or even before you get out of bed in the morning, write down a Stoic saying that you think will be helpful for what's to come. Commit that saying to memory, then write a short summary of it in your own words, and a bit about how you think it applies to your situation. Carry the journal, paper, or book in which you wrote the saying with you and, when you can, write down the times throughout the day where it was pertinent, and whether or not you think you lived up to your interpretation of it. Then, at the end of the day, review what you wrote. Upon reflection, did your original interpretation of the passage prove true? If so, where did you meet the challenge it issued? Where did you fail? If not, how would you alter your interpretation to better accord with your experience? Write these meditations down and refer to them again the next time that particular piece of wisdom is relevant.

Try having a conversation with yourself from the future. Say you think of yourself at the end of your Stoic exercises. Think of the kinds of qualities you would like yourself to have, the kinds of virtues you would like yourself to exercise, the kind of disposition you would like yourself to cultivate. If you, as a time traveler, went forward to meet this version of yourself and ask about your current troubles, what would that you say? What advice would they give on how to deal with the annoying colleague, the stressful job, or the frightening turn of events? Bringing these concrete situations to the ideal you is akin to the next exercise, which I consider a superior version because it challenges you to not just think of a better version of yourself but of a virtuous person tout court, exercising your understanding of the virtues at the same time that it calls you to practical, meditative activity. Which version you prefer, however, may be different, so I offer both and leave it open for you to decide.

Let's consider a final exercise in the anticipatory framework, then, examining values. Imagine the qualities of a virtuous person. In what sorts of situations are they kind, philanthropic, well-tempered? How would they endure the challenges awaiting you? Now imagine the vicious person. Where do they fall short? How would they handle your challenges? Write down some key qualities you think describe these people. These are your guiding attributes. As Epictetus says in his *Enchiridion*,

"Immediately prescribe some character and form of conduce to yourself, which you may keep both alone and in company."[29]

We can also heed the words of Marcus Aurelius in book six of his Meditations when he says:

"When thou wishest to delight thyself, think of the virtues of those who live with thee; for instance, the activity of one, and the modesty of another, and the liberality of a third, and some other good quality of a fourth. For nothing delights so much as the examples of the virtues, when they are exhibited in the morals of those who live with us and present themselves in abundance, as far as is possible. Wherefore we must keep them before us."

Through the day, take note of situations in which you tend toward the virtuous or the viscous person. Your goal is to learn what kind of situations you should meet and what kind you should avoid. Further, for those situations that test you or in which you tend toward viscous qualities—toward intemperance, cowardice, or injustice—take note of how you fall short, and suggest for yourself what you can do to overcome these hardships. Once you've finished your day,

---

29 Epictetus, *Enchiridion*

flip the page, start a new entry, or even grab a new notebook if you must! You should treat each day as a new experience, as a new opportunity to meet your goals, and you should also make a new list and set new goals as your thoughts evolve. And when you're ready, review your progress over the last week or month. You'll be surprised at how far you can develop in a short time.

"Preventative measures are all good," you might tell me, "but what about when I am in the moment?" In the end, the exercise of virtue comes down to a moment-to-moment, situation-to-situation decisions. In the next chapter, let's look at some Stoic exercises for dealing with our problems as they arise, and for reflecting upon them after they have passed.

Stoic Discomfort

The Stoics see one's approach to misfortune as crucial to a life of tranquility. Suffering can take on many forms, from damaged property to damaged relationships, to death. Our poor circumstances, the Stoics think, breed opportunities to practice virtue. It is a central tenant of Stoic practice that one is strengthened whenever they handle unfortunate situations in a thoughtful and disciplined way. Of course, one does not seek misfortune for the sake of practice, but it is not necessary to anyway. Even minor slights, petty disagreements, and minute irritants can help us develop our habits and our faculty of choice in a way that is in accordance with nature, that contributes to human flourishing. In this chapter I will discuss daily discomforts in the context of Stoic practice, to show you ways you can cope with unfortunate events, both great and small.

Imagine you are in your favorite restaurant, about to enjoy your favorite dish. You smell the seasoning, admire the color, feel the texture, savor the taste. And when the meal is done, you are left wanting more; you are even upset that it did not last longer. So what do you do? You pay your check and leave the restaurant. But you enjoyed yourself so much, how could you possibly walk away without ordering more? There could be many practical reasons. The dish is expensive, you are already full, you have an appointment. But another reason is that you know, fate permitting, this isn't the last time you'll taste good food. You enjoyed the meal, but you are not singularly attached to that experience at that time. You don't feel an immediate need to repeat it.

This above attitude is akin to how the Stoics think we should treat enjoyments. When we experience any pleasure, we should not be carried away by it. We should not allow ourselves to lose control of our emotions. Their reasoning is twofold. First, they think a resigned attitude toward pleasure is also practiced for when we confront pain. Epictetus says in his *Enchiridion*,

"If you are struck by the appearance of any promised pleasure, guard yourself against being hurried away by it; but let the affair wait for your leisure, and procure yourself some delay. Then bring to your mind both points of time: that in which you will enjoy the pleasure, and that in which you will repent and reproach yourself after you have enjoyed it; and set before you, in opposition to these, how you will be glad and applaud yourself if you abstain. And even though it should appear to you a seasonable gratification, take heed that its enticing, and agreeable and attractive force may not subdue you; but set in opposition to this how much better it is to be conscious of having gained so great a victory."[30]

If, after all, you cannot control yourself during enjoyment, how can you expect to enjoy yourself when you're suffering, when it may be more difficult to maintain discipline? Emperor Marcus Aurelius speaks of the temptation of sleep in particular. In book five of his *Meditations*, he says,

"In the morning when thou risest unwillingly, let this thought be present- I am rising to the work of a human being. Why then am I dissatisfied if I am going to do the things for which I exist and for which I was brought into the world? Or have I been made for this, to lie in the bed-clothes and keep myself warm?- But this is more pleasant.- Dost thou exist then to take thy pleasure, and not at all for action or exertion? Dost thou does not see the little plants, the little birds, the ants, the spiders, the bees working together to put in order their several parts of the universe? And art thou unwilling to do the work of a human being, and dost thou do not make haste to do that which is according to thy nature?"[31]

---

30   Epictetus, *Enchiridion*
31   Marcus Aurelius, *Meditations*, book five

Second, they think you are thereby asserting control over your emotions. Epictetus says that we should make our impressions wait for us, rather than the other way around. Know that you are just fine without experiencing any given sensation, that you have control over it, and you will find it becomes easier to restrain yourself when it matters.

But how do we measure when restraint is appropriate and to what degree it is appropriate? Epictetus says we should measure our actions within the context of our relationships and our situation. If your sibling harms you, you do not cut ties with them, not only because you might one day need a kidney, but also because familial relationships are within our closest circle of concern. These are the people most important to us. But if an acquaintance wrongs you, though you should not lose your temper or concern yourself with actions that are not your own, you are under no obligation to continue interacting with that person. In fact, if they prove to be a continual irritant, and if they themselves are vicious, the Stoics recommend you cease contact. In both situations, your response is in proportion to the care you can and should be expected to show toward that person. Similarly, when dealing with pleasures and pains, act in accordance with sound judgment, in proportion to the impression under question.

The Stoics call upon us to live consistently. If you think someone else should behave a certain way, whether it is by showing patience, restraining their fear, or being just in their exchanges with others, ask yourself whether or not you are also living up to that principle. If you are not, or if there are situations in which you have fallen short in the past, do not expect another person to be better than you are. By looking at people in the context of our own abilities, we temper our expectations and eschew pain arising from their shortcomings.

I think the best way to ensure your expectations align with your abilities, and with what can be expected from others, is to engage in Stoic meditations. Meditation for the Stoics is not like it is in Buddhism; it does not involve clearing your mind and accepting impressions as they arise and pass away. Stoic meditation is an active process in which you evaluate your actions and ideas, dig through them for those attitudes you will keep and those you will discard. We can split the list of questions you should ask yourself into two, one following Epictetus' example, the other following Seneca's.

Before looking at the kinds of questions each of these thinkers would have you ask, consider a broader inquiry. Ask yourself what you did wrong today. Which of your actions do you accept, which do you condemn? Also, ask what virtue and strength you've shown today. Were your actions consistent with your nature as a rational subject? What can you do to realign them? Finally, ask what you can do better. You may not be correcting follies here, but looking for situations in which you could have exercised virtue, in which you could have gone beyond neutral activity.

Once you have answered these general questions, consider the kinds of questions Epictetus would ask himself. Did you go wrong in any way that hinders your serenity or personal flourishing? Did you attribute blame to those who did not deserve it, or take umbrage at some event or circumstance not under your control? What did you do that was antisocial, inconsiderate, or unfriendly? Did you, to your fullest extent, exercise justice with respect to others? If not, what duties did you abrogate in your relationships? What effect do you think your actions will have on others, and, in the long term, what damage have you done to yourself? These questions behind you, let us not turn to Seneca, who asks a similar, but distinct, set of questions.

Seneca draws his questions from the meditations of Sextus Empericus. Before he would close his eyes and fall asleep, the latter would ask himself three things. First, which of your evils have you cured today? This question was a call to account for moral development, a measure of his progress toward virtuous living. Second, which of your vices have you fought? In other words, which of your bad habits did you target, and where did you succeed or fail in overcoming them. Finally, how are you better? Is there any sense in which you have improved yourself and, if not, how can you change your behaviors to make a difference in your character tomorrow?

If you give yourself an honest account, you can take, to what extent it is possible, an objective view of yourself and your failings. But it is also important to praise yourself when you do well. To do so is to treat yourself both as a friend and a wise counselor. The idea of these questions, and of taking a Stoic view toward your failings, is to apply the theoretical aspects of Stoic doctrine, in order to live a fuller and more consistent life. A life worthy of human nature.

Apatheia — Stoic Inner Peace

For the Stoics, the center of eudaimonia, human flourishing, is apatheia, being without passions. I have said before that this, despite being the Hellenistic root of our English word apathy, does not mean indifference or insensitivity. Apatheia Is to be thought of in relation to our earlier discussion of emotional mastery. For the Stoics, it is the name of that state that arises when one has been thoroughly dyed in virtue. And, crucially for us, it is the end goal of Stoic training and exercises. In a word, the good life is one in which the state of apatheia is the core of right choices in ethical action.

When the Stoics use the term passion, they do not mean only emotion. To be more precise, the Stoic passions, as we saw in the chapter on CBT, can be either healthy or unhealthy. Examples of unhealthy passions include fear, pain, pleasure, and cravings. Healthy passions include caution, discretion, delight and willing. Caution and discretion are the opposites of fear, delight is the opposite of pleasure, willing is the opposite of craving. Pain does not have an opposite that is still a "passion" in the Stoic sense of the term. As you can see, the Stoic passions are not quite emotions. It is more correct to say that they are affections of the soul.

The passions are in a way instinctive reactions, the experience of which we cannot avoid. They result from a kind of assent given to impressions. We saw an example of this assent with respect to fear, where the initial shock of an encounter became fear when one reflected upon and chose to designate it an evil. It is not correct to identify fear as the initial fight-or-flight response to a perceived danger. Once it is or has become subject to your control, once it is presented to your soul, to your faculty of choice, then it is a passion in the proper sense.

Pain considered as a passion for the Stoics in a sense mirrors the Epicurean meaning of the word. For the Epicureans, pains were not just the feeling of discomfort, but a feeling whose origin was in a choice, specifically the failure to choose to avoid something. For the Stoics, too, pain is not just the feeling of hurt or injury, but also an irrational expectation. To be sure cutting oneself on a piece of glass is a pain in part of its sense, just as being startled is part of the meaning is fear. But these initial or involuntary reactions do not capture the full meanings of the words and for that reason the Stoics the limited senses of the words from those senses which involve what is fully us, our decision making core. As Emperor Marcus Aurelius says in book nine of his *Meditations*,

"Thou canst remove out of the way many useless things among those which disturb thee, for they lie entirely in thy opinion; and thou wilt then gain for thyself ample space by comprehending the whole universe in thy mind, and by contemplating the eternity of time, and observing the rapid change of every several thing, how short is the time from birth to dissolution, and the illimitable time before birth as well as the equally boundless time after dissolution."[32]

Apatheia is a state in which these unhealthy passions are turned on their heads. In the examples given above, one who is affected by Stoic apatheia, instead of experiencing fear, experiences a sense caution. One who would experience an intense craving, an irrational striving for something mistakenly judged as good, instead experiences wishing, a rational desire for virtue. One who would be subject to pleasure, an irrational elation over something that is actually not worth choosing, would instead experience joy or delight, a rational elation over virtue. By their very phrasing, "rational elation over virtue," etc., you can see that these dispositions are a kind of habituation, an inner discipline or well-developed faculty of choice that governs both our reactions to

---

[32] Marcus Aurelius, *Meditations,* book nine

these passions and those objects that excite our passions to begin with.

Apatheia also yields a second state, one at which the Epicureans in their pursuit of pleasure aimed directly, ataraxia. Ataraxia means "imperturbability" or literally being without trouble or tranquility. For the Epicureans, this meant that, through prudent living and correct choices, one relieved themselves of pain, this being for them the greatest sort of pleasure or the limit of pleasure. For the Stoics, it means living a life in accordance with one's nature, which means a life of virtue. Such a life is directed toward its aims — it accomplishes its goals and is thereby brought into tranquility, even if that tranquility leads one through what are otherwise discomforts like engaging in social or political life, an aspect of human experience that the Epicureans recommended we avoid at all cost.

This brings us at last to one final idea, that of Stoic cosmopolitanism. Indeed, if there is any rational opposite of misdirected passion in politics, it is this notion. For the Stoics, the aim of political life is securing the reproduction and improvement of public virtue. In book nine of his *Meditations*, Marcus Aurelius says:

"As thou thyself art a component part of a social system, so let every act of thine be a component part of social life. Whatever act of thine then has no reference either immediately or remotely to a social end, this tears asunder thy life, and does not allow it to be one, and it is of the nature of a mutiny, just as when in a popular assembly a man acting by himself stands apart from the general agreement."[33]

Public virtue is the opposite of private virtue in the sense that the latter has only the well-being of the self as its end while the former sees the exercise of virtue in context. The case is easy enough with justice. When one engages with others such that obligations are upheld, and when this becomes a general rule, society is more cohesive. What of courage or temperance? Is society not improved when individuals endure difficult circumstances and take only what satisfies their needs? When virtue is directed toward civic improvement when philosophical practice is also political practice, the individual benefits as well as the polity.

Here too Stoic practice meets its pedagogical ends. By living a life according to virtue, by developing apatheia as a disposition, one serves as a living example of their theoretical

---

33   Marcus Aurelius, *Meditations,* book nine

commitments. And this active life of spreading philosophy, as we saw at the very beginning of this book, is the aim of philosophy as a discipline. Mastery of the passions, then, is a necessary condition for the spreading of Stoic ideas, insofar as those ideas flourish when they are lived. Remember here the words of Epictetus from his *Enchiridion*:

"And, if anyone tells you that you know nothing, and you are not nettled at it, then you may be sure that you have begun your business. For sheep don't throw up the grass to show the shepherds how much they have eaten; but, inwardly digesting their food, they outwardly produce wool and milk. Thus, therefore, do you likewise not show theorems to the unlearned, but the actions produced by them after they have been digested."[34]

---

34   Epictetus, *Enchiridion*

Conclusion

Stoicism as an ethical system brings together logic, physics, ethics, and psychology to paint a picture of the whole human being. I hope I have, in this book, presented its ideas in a clear, digestible format pleasing to both the eyes and the mind.

It is no secret that Stoicism's survival, its flourishing, and its rebirth are due to its malleability and the applicability of its doctrines. Epictetus says often that it is not enough to know Stoic doctrine, one must also practice, to develop habits, if they want to master its ideas and understand it in practice.

When I first encountered Stoicism, it was as an undergraduate in college. At the time I had very little interest in philosophy as a whole outside of those goals which served my ego—having the upper hand in arguments, justifying my beliefs, and adding another chip to my shoulder. Stoicism did not at the time appeal to me. I should have heeded Epictetus' words when he says in the *Enchiridion*,

"Never call yourself a philosopher, nor talk a great deal among the unlearned about theorems, but act conformably to them. Thus, at an entertainment, don't talk how persons ought to eat, but eat as you ought. For remember that in this manner Socrates also universally avoided all ostentation. And when persons came to him and desired to be recommended by him to philosophers, he took and- recommended them, so well did he bear being overlooked."[35]

It was several years, and a bit more engagement with philosophy, before the value of Stoicism became evident. Its treatment of the human being as a whole, engaging both the nature of the mind and its relationship to social responsibility, is not unique in philosophy, but no other individual philosophy can claim to have had such a far-reaching impact on the lives of people not wading through the theoretical reeds.

I think it is this accessibility, deeply connected to the breadth of its applicability, that explains its success. Whether dealing with trouble in the workplace, at home, or in one's own heart, Stoicism is a well of wisdom whose wealth has been drawn consistently for thousands of years. Whether considering what one controls, or how to apply what is controlled and what is not (for example the relationship between what is in our power and what is assigned to us as a duty, like the rearing of our children), or the application of virtue in ethical life.

---

[35] Epictetus, *Enchiridion*

The Stoic sage is untroubled by that which they cannot control, but also capable of boundless compassion for friends and family, country, and the whole of humanity. This principle of Stoic concern is called cosmopolitanism; it is intimately connected with the idea that we are citizens of the world. Further, it draws upon the idea of Divine Fire we discussed earlier. We are all sparks of creation, the force that moves all of creation also moves us. It is for this reason that we must recognize ourselves and our motivations as situated in an interconnected whole, one damaged when we fail to treat one another with respect and compassion.

Stoic compassion is a central theme, as maybe you've gleaned from this book. As I've said before, the Stoics are the opposite of insensible, despite this being one of their popular reputations. Their doctrines are infused with care for those who deserve it, charity for those who need it, and understanding for those who fail in their responsibilities. With respect to duty, especially duties concerning those in our care, the Stoics entreat us to show due attention, but also warn us against passion. This is not an idle doctrine. What care is appropriate to the maintenance of what has been loaned to us by fortune is both the limit of our attachment and the appropriate attitude to see it preserved. Passion, on the other hand, is the cousin of exuberance and overreaction and, even in the

It is said that the great Emperor Marcus Aurelius was a fortress of these attitudes. Can you imagine, the most powerful man in the world, one with absolute authority over life and death in the entire known world, living a life in service to those beneath him? We live with minor temptations. Whether or not to cheat on our taxes, to shoplift a beverage, to cheat on our spouse. How much more must this temptation be for one with absolute impunity? Who could get away with any crime, have any woman, appropriate all the wealth in the world if he so desired? We know that other Roman emperors were not able to resist their temptations. But it is evidence of the power of Stoic ideas that The Stoic Emperor would be the superior of those that preceded him and those that followed.

We can follow his example. If he, with all his might, could resist his temptations, I think we have hope. In truth, what Stoic doctrines ask of us is not grand. After all, many of us already record our thoughts in journals, logs, and stories. In the west, we are obsessed with data. Everything from our heart rate to our calorie intake, to the number of steps we take is already recorded. Recording our moral development is not too far a stretch! I think, at any rate, the information recorded is more useful than a record of the number of carbs we've consumed. As for its difficulty, we should remember the words of Epictetus from chapter twelve, book three of his *Discourses*. There he says:

"Everything, which is difficult and dangerous is not suitable for practice; but that is suitable which conduces to the working out of that which is proposed to us as a thing to be worked out. To live with desire and aversion, free from restraint. And what is this? Neither to be disappointed in that which you desire nor to fall into anything which you would avoid. Toward this object, then, exercise ought to tend. For, since it is not possible to have your desire not disappointed and your aversion free from falling into that which you would avoid, great and constant practice you must know that if you allow your desire and aversion to turn to things which are not within the power of the will, you will neither have your desire capable of attaining your object, nor your aversion free from the power of avoiding that which you would avoid."[36]

Just like the other information we keep track of, there is a wealth of opportunity for social engagement in Stoic self-evaluation. Already numerous groups, blogs, and

---

36   Epictetus, *Discourses,* book three, chapter twelve

communities have formed online and around the world filled with like-minded people focused on the improvement of themselves and their communities. Modern Stoicism is alive and growing. This book, too, is an entry in a revived philosophical movement. I hope you use it as a gateway. Though I've tried to cover all aspects of Stoicism to some extent, each topic touched on here is far more complex than I could field between these pages. By engaging with others, by sharing your experiences and your failings, you will uncover a mountain of practical advice aimed both at expanding on the ideas discussed here and on troubleshooting them. As with anything, Stoicism takes work. The dispositions outlined here may be at times difficult to wrap your head around, at other times their applicability might not be immediately obvious, but studying and understanding them is preparation for possible experiences. Experiences that others have had, and that you, too, might one day encounter.

It has been a joy and a pleasure taking the plunge with you and being your guide. I hope you also enjoyed the experience. Remember that Stoicism is half theoretical, half practical. It is possible that many misunderstandings will remain even after years of study. As with any sufficiently complex philosophical theory, there is always something new to discover, some new aspect or way of reading the text to uncover. With Stoicism especially, finding these new readings will require you to live the doctrine, and also teach others. You do not, of course, have to sit down with them and go over the details of Stoic virtue. Rather, you should live Stoic teachings, and teach by example in turn. Through consistent and engaged activity, you'll not only find your own life improved but also the lives of your loved ones—both inside and out.

Bibliography

Epictetus. *The Enchiridion*. Translated by Elizabeth Carter.

http://classics.mit.edu/Epictetus/epicench.html.

Aurelius, Marcus. *Meditations*. Translated by George Long.

http://classics.mit.edu/Antoninus/meditations.html.

Cicero, Marcus T. *On Duties*. Translated by Cyrus R. Edmonds. New York, NY: Harper & Brothers, 1855.

https://archive.org/stream/cicerosthreebook00cicerich/cicerosthreebook00cicerich_djvu.txt.

Epictetus. *Discourses*.

http://classics.mit.edu/Epictetus/discourses.html.

Description

Tag line: Stoicism, one of the oldest, Western philosophical schools, has enchanted scholars and the general public alike for over two thousand years. Where some accounts of human nature and the particularly human good fall short by the reduction of human being to physical or psychical phenomena, Stoicism's power lies in engaging with the whole range of human experience, addressing rationality, emotion, piety, will, and both inner and outer impressions, each on their own terms, in language that treats each as significant in its own right.

This book is a general introduction to Stoicism that pulls no punches when faced with the more complex aspects of Stoic doctrine. Topics addressed include:

- -The history of the ancient Stoics.
- -The nature of good and evil, virtue and vice, and positive and negative externals.
- -The difference between those things in our control and those things not in our control.
- -Stoic Logic and practical reasoning.

- -Stoicism's role in the development of cognitive behavioral therapy (CBT).
- -Stoic exercises and daily practice.
- -Theology's role in Stoicism and Stoic cosmology.
- And much more!

Stoicism is an active philosophy. That means that it is not enough to know its doctrines, one must also live them, develop habits that expand on and complete their ideas in practice. Practice, therefore, is also the focus of this book. The development of the reader's inner and outer life, that they may follow their own path and discover what it means to "live life in accordance with nature."

www.ingramcontent.com/pod-product-compliance
Lightning Source LLC
Chambersburg PA
CBHW071739080526
44588CB00013B/2092